DRUIDS, GODS & HEROES
from
CELTIC MYTHOLOGY

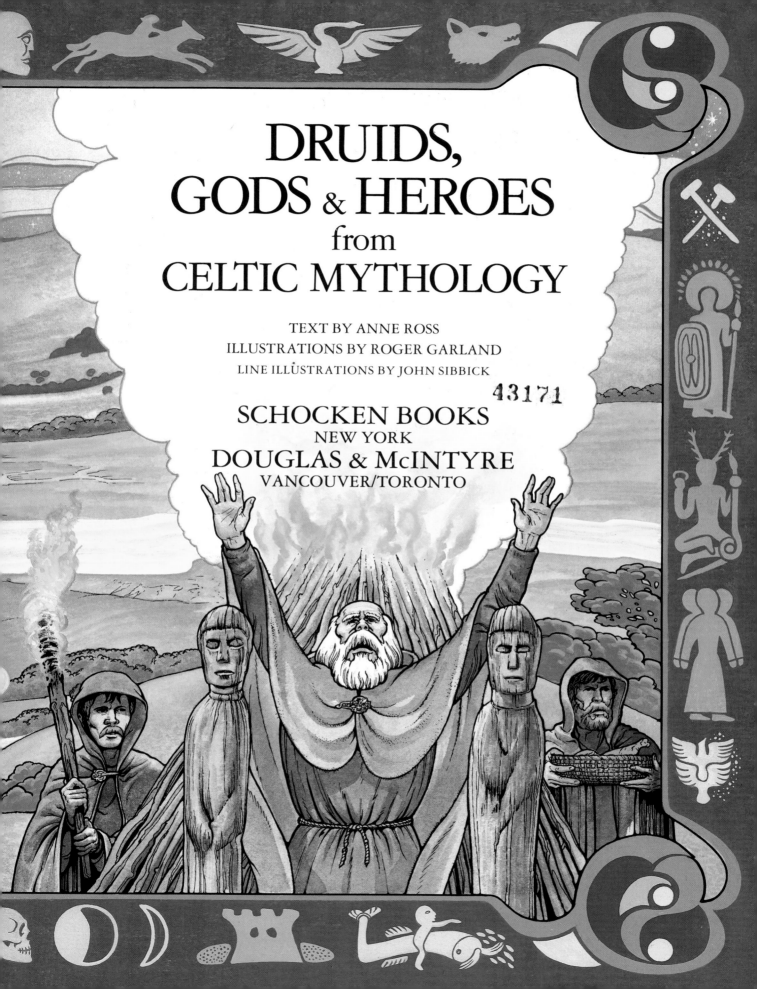

DRUIDS, GODS & HEROES
from
CELTIC MYTHOLOGY

TEXT BY ANNE ROSS

ILLUSTRATIONS BY ROGER GARLAND

LINE ILLUSTRATIONS BY JOHN SIBBICK

SCHOCKEN BOOKS
NEW YORK

DOUGLAS & McINTYRE
VANCOUVER/TORONTO

First American edition published
by Schocken Books 1986
10 9 8 7 6 5 4 3 2 1 86 87 88 89
Library of Congress Cataloging-
in-Publication Data
Ross, Anne, Ph.D.
    Druids, gods and heroes from
    Celtic mythology.
    1. Mythology, Celtic. I. Title.
BL900.R59 1986 299'.16 85-29444

ISBN 0-8052-4014-4 (Schocken)

Published in Canada by
Douglas & McIntyre Ltd.
1615 Venables Street
Vancouver, British Columbia

Canadian Cataloguing in
Publication Data
    Ross, Anne, Ph.D.
    Druids, gods and heroes from
    Celtic mythology
    (World mythologies series)
    Includes index.
    1. Mythology, Celtic -
    Juvenile literature.
    I. Title. II. Series.
BL900.R59 1986 j299'.16
C86-091052-0

ISBN 0-88894-510-8 (Douglas & McIntyre)

Manufactured in Italy

THE AUTHOR
Dr Anne Ross has specialized in the culture of the
ancient Celtic peoples and translates fluently from
early Welsh, Irish, Scottish and French texts. She is a
Research Fellow at the University of Southampton,
England and is one of the leading authorities on the
Celtic world. She is the author of many books and
articles including *Pagan Celtic Britain* and *Everyday
Life of the Pagan Celts*.

THE ARTISTS
Roger Garland studied art and graphic design at
both Plymouth and Wolverhampton Colleges of Art
and is a full-time illustrator. His speciality is fantasy
and he has produced cover illustrations for many of
the books of J R Tolkien and illustrated a Tolkien
calendar.

John Sibbick studied art at Guildford School of
Art and is also a full-time painter and illustrator. He
specializes in accurate reconstructions of life in the
past and has illustrated a number of books, both
fiction and non-fiction.

Contents

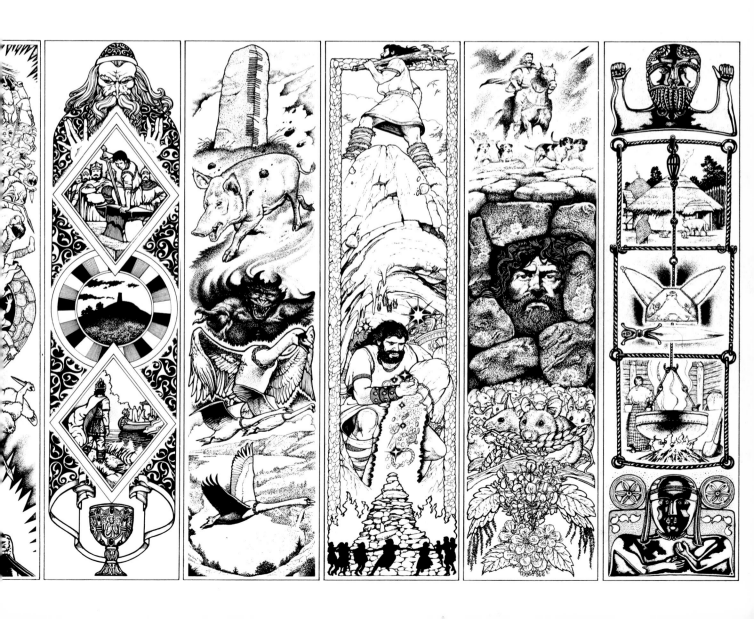

The ancient Celtic world

The Celts were the true creators of Europe, the ancestors of all modern Europeans. At the height of their power in about 300 BC they occupied and dominated all the land from the Baltic to the Mediterranean and from the Black Sea to the turbulent western shores of Ireland. By race they were Indo-Europeans, a people who occupied the region north of the Black Sea, and who at some time about 2500 BC began to spread out throughout Europe and eastwards towards India. From their languages most European languages and some Indian dialects developed.

The name Celtic was not recorded until Herodotus, the Greek historian, mentioned them in the fifth century BC. By then they were a great and powerful people, composed of tribes with different names but knowing themselves collectively as *Keltoi* and bound together by common political organization, a powerful priesthood, religious traditions, languages and appearance. Their culture, however, began much earlier and it would not be fanciful to say that the origins of the Celtic world reach back to the third millenium BC.

Archaeologists divide the early phases of Celtic prehistory into Hallstatt (c.700-500 BC) and La Tène (c.500—1st century AD). The names come from sites in Austria and Switzerland respectively where many ancient objects have been found. The Hallstatt Celts grew rich and powerful with their discovery and skilful use of iron, a metal far superior to that used by their Bronze Age ancestors. It made much more formidable weapons, superior cutting-tools, vessels and utensils of all kinds. In 600 BC a Celtic colony was established at Massilia, now Marseille, and trade was successfully developed with the Mediterranean countries. As the chieftains grew richer, their new technology and the objects they made using it spread widely throughout Europe, bringing with it great cultural advances.

By 500 BC the scene had been set for the emergence of the formidable and passionate La Tène Celts who, with their light, two-wheeled, iron-tyred war-chariots, were to sweep with relentless speed and skill through Europe, conquering the Etruscans, settling the Italian peninsula, parts of Greece and Asia Minor (Galatia), and travelling as far west as the Iberian Peninsula and the British Isles.

People were terrified of them and yet filled with admiration for their technological skills, their exquisite artwork, and their religious fervour and passion for learning. In 390 BC they successfully sacked Rome and in 279 BC a Celtic tribe from Asia Minor, the Galatae, attacked the Greek city of Delphi. The attack on Delphi failed but the Celts remained in the Balkans. Some of them were mercenary soldiers known as 'the spear bearers' who served under many leaders, including Alexander the Great and must have travelled far and wide, probably even as far as China.

In 225 BC their power began to crumble when a huge army of Celts from Gaul was trapped at Telamon north of Rome by two Roman armies and routed. From then on, the Celts' supremacy in Europe gradually declined, although it was over 200 years before Julius Caesar finally conquered Gaul in 58 BC and almost another hundred before a large part of Britain was incorporated within the Roman Empire.

But the story does not end with the conquest by Rome. The Celts continued to exist all over Europe, and although the languages died out in most areas, their ideas, their superstitions and their folk festivals and place-names survived. Ireland and much of Scotland were never conquered and there, in Wales and in the Isle of Man, Celtic culture continued to exist, retaining its art, its religion and its language. Cornwall also remained her Celtic self, although the Romans mined for tin and built villas there. Later, in the fifth and sixth centuries AD, Cornish and Welsh settlers returned to mainland Europe, bringing Celtic traditions back to Brittany.

The Celtic druid-king Diviciacus was a close personal friend of Julius Caesar and stayed with him in Rome; when Caesar wrote about the structure of Celtic society, he was therefore almost certainly using first-hand information. He recorded that there were two classes of men of some dignity and importance. The common people were regarded nearly as slaves. One of the two classes was that of the druids, the other that of the knights. The druids were concerned with the worship of the gods, looked after public and private sacrifice and expounded religious matters. They had the right to decide nearly all public and private disputes and they also passed judgement and decided rewards and penalties in criminal and murder cases and in disputes concerning legacies and boundaries. When a private person or a tribe disobeyed their ruling they banned them from attending at sacrifices. This was a very harsh penalty since it made the banned person an outlaw, with no rights in the tribe.

The druids had a chief who held authority over them. When he died, either the highest in honour among the others succeeded or if the choice was difficult, a vote was taken or even a fight arranged. At a fixed time of the year they met in assembly in a holy place which was regarded as the centre of the whole of Gaul. Anyone who had a dispute to be resolved came and accepted the druids' decision.

The ancient site of the druids' meeting in Gaul may have been where Chartres Cathedral stands today. In Ireland, an equivalent druidic shrine was at Tara while the Island of Anglesey was the centre of druidism for Britain.

Caesar reported that the druids learned by heart immense amounts of poetry. Some of them continued their studies for twenty years. They considered it improper to use writing in their studies although they used the Greek alphabet in nearly everything else, in their public and private accounts.

One of the druids' main religious tasks was to convince the people that souls are never destroyed, but after death pass from one body to another. This was regarded as the strongest incentive to bravery since it helped the warriors to overcome the fear of death. Another Roman writer described how effective this teaching was. Some of the Celts, he said, so far despised death that they went into battle unclothed except for a girdle. When the opposing armies were drawn up in battle lines, the warriors would advance in front of the chariots, challenging the bravest of the enemy to single combat and brandishing their swords and javelins to bring terror to their hearts.

Caesar also recorded that the druids had considerable knowledge of the stars and their motion, of the size of the world and of the earth, of natural philosophy, and of the powers and spheres of action of the immortal gods.

The Celtic tribes lived in such widely different regions that daily life must have varied with climate, soil type, how near they were to the sea and other factors but archaeological evidence shows that their overall way of life was basically the same. They lived in hill forts or fortified houses on low ground. The houses, some extremely large, were circular, with heavy domed, thatched roofs. On the mainland of Europe the houses could also be oval or square, but in Britain and Ireland they were usually round. They were not interested in architecture, but preferred the comfort of their warm houses, usually with a central fire and a smoke-hole through the thatch. A long chain suspended above the fire held a great cooking cauldron and spits for the roasting of joints.

They made bread in ovens or on griddles and they also had cooking pits in the ground in which whole animals could be roasted. They drank milk, ale and mead, and wine when they could get it. Fresh and salted pork was the favourite food at the feast, also fish seasoned with cumin and salmon baked in honey. Cheese was made and herbs were used for seasoning as well as for medicine. They grew woad in order to make a blue dye, and used other vegetable dyes for colouring cloth.

Although their homes were not luxurious by Mediterranean standards, the knights, druids and wealthy freemen lived well. They were a vain people, proud of their luxuriant hair and bleaching it fairer with lime and adorning it with baubles of gold. Gold was more plentiful in the western Celtic world, silver in the east. Their parade weapons were elaborately fashioned and decorated with precious metals and jewels and their houses were adorned with rich carvings of red yew. The walls of their feasting halls were hung with patterned silks and linens and their clothing woven with gold threads and borders, and with a variety of checks and stripes. The descriptions of their neck ornaments, armlets, anklets, rings, head-dresses and helmets in the tales are confirmed by the finds of archaeology.

The Gauls favoured trousers: the Irish, tunics. All wore cloaks and the length of these showed the wearer's rank. Favourite pursuits were hunting, cattle-raiding, warring, feasting, playing board games and above all, listening to music and poetry and tales, and worshipping the capricious gods. Religion dominated their lives. Things must be observed, acknowledged, or avoided. Tabus were placed on those in authority and to break them meant destruction.

There were many gods and goddesses throughout the wider Celtic world most known to us only through inscriptions, place-names, Roman references and, above all, through the tales which have survived in the Celtic world of Ireland and Wales. The Celts had a long oral tradition which their learned men cherished and the stories they told of their gods and heroes reflect an ancient way of life that must have been common all over Europe. It is from them that we learn of the old traditions of law, the concepts of kingship, of truth and of the 'fitness of things' which held their society together.

Perhaps the best known of all Celtic heroes is Arthur, the only Celt whose name is a household word throughout Europe and Europe's former colonies. His legendary adventures take place in both Britain and France and he is said to lie sleeping beneath Mount Etna in Sicily, an island that was settled by Celts at the height of their power in Europe. In France he was known as 'le roi Artus' and his name may have come from a god named Artaios who was compared by the Romans to their own god Mercury. By the Middle Ages King Arthur was thought to be a real, historical figure; but it is possible that the stories about him that were passed down from generation to generation and from tribe to tribe were once told about a powerful god known under different names throughout the whole of Celtic Europe.

The stories in this book have been retold from the original old Irish and Welsh tales, the oldest surviving written literature in Europe apart from Greek and Roman. Through them and through the festivals and folklore that still remain, a dim memory has been kept alive of what were once the deeply held beliefs and practices of our ancestors in Europe.

The arrival of the gods

The Book of Invasions (*Lebor Gabala* in Irish) was compiled by Irish scholars in the twelfth century. It is a work of great importance in which much genuine history, as well as invaluable mythology, is embedded. The entire text begins with the arrival of Partholon and his people in Ireland after the Flood, but that part is not included here. We begin with the conquest of Nemed, one of the Greeks living in Scythia. The Scythians were a nomadic people who lived some five hundred miles north-east of Greece, in the lands bordering the Caspian Sea. They had close cultural affinities with the Celts, especially in their exquisite art, in their custom of tattooing the body and in their random domestic arrangements. Their contacts with the Greeks and the Graeco-Celts must have been very close, as the Book of Invasions implies and the original text uses the terms Greece and Scythia interchangeably. Taken at its face value as a historical document, the Book of Invasions is virtually worthless but used judiciously as a source for history and mythology, it is a true treasure-trove.

The stories of the four invasions must have been passed on by word of mouth for many, many generations before they were written down and although they may record a memory of actual events, the characters and incidents have become transformed until men, gods and monsters are marvellously intermingled. The scholars who finally wrote them down were convinced that they were writing a true historical document; what they produced was far more than that, a record of the earliest myths of the Irish Celts and an insight into the old beliefs of all the Celtic people. All the action in the book leads up to the final invasion and conquest by the Gaels of the land that is destined through divine intervention to be in their possession for ever after.

The first invasion of Ireland is known as The conquest of Nemed. It takes place at a time before Ireland had settled into its permanent form, when it was a wild, dangerous place, ravaged by sickness and inhabited only by a tribe of monstrous people, the Fomorians. The Fomorians, who appear as sinister, supernatural people, figure largely in the Book. Their name includes the Celtic words for 'sea' and 'under', so is translated as 'those who live under the sea'.

Nemed, it was said, came from Greece long ago, making the perilous journey westwards to find a new home for his people. A great plague had left Ireland empty and desolate for some thirty years before the arrival of Nemed and his followers. They had set sail in a fleet of thirty-four oared boats with thirty people in each vessel. The sea was calm and the winds favourable and all went well until they saw a golden tower jutting out of the water close by them. Its smooth yellow walls glistened in the sea mist and its top was so high that it was lost in the clouds.

Hoping to find treasure there, the fleet rowed towards it but around the tower there surged treacherous and violent currents which capsized many of the ships and drove others onto jagged underwater rocks. Only Nemed's boat survived and almost all those travelling with him were drowned. But Nemed himself, his children and the few people he could rescue from the water were saved. The survivors sailed away from the mysterious tower and came at last to the shores of Ireland. Here they settled but their troubles were not at an end: only twelve days after they had landed, Nemed's wife Macha became the first to die there when she fell victim to the plague which still ravaged the land.

Overseas to the north of Ireland lived a fierce tribe known as the Fomorians. They, too, were anxious to settle in Ireland, but Nemed and his men were too strong for them and set them to work as slaves. Their labour began to change the face of the country, for they built two great royal forts and carved out twelve wide plains from the forested land. The landscape was also still changing from natural causes in those days and it was during the time of Nemed that four mighty cloudbursts formed the four great lakes of Ireland, the same lakes that can still be seen today.

While Nemed lived, he was able to control the sullen, rebellious Fomorians, although he lost many of his own men in the three battles he fought to subdue them; but eventually he, too, became ill and died of the plague that still lurked in corners of Ireland.

Now the monstrous Fomorians saw their chance to defeat the Children of Nemed and without Nemed to lead them, they were soon overcome. The Fomorians were cruel overlords. Every year at the festival of Samain (Hallowe'en) they compelled the Children of Nemed to give them two-thirds of their corn, two-thirds of their milk produce and two-thirds of their new-born infants, a terrible tax. The Children of Nemed were enraged by this heavy toll and plotted to get the better of their oppressors. They sent abroad for foreign soldiers, strangers and even criminals to enlist their aid, and they also despatched messengers to their kinsmen in Greece asking for assistance.

A great company set sail for Ireland, a company which included many druids and druidesses as well as the finest warriors. They also brought with them vicious animals including wolves and venomous pigs. The fleet anchored at the place where Conann, the king of the Fomorians, lived in his tower of glass and laid siege to it so that Conann was forced to give battle to this mighty, magical army.

First the druids and druidesses of each army competed against each other, employing all their powers of enchantment and illusion. However, for every spell there was a counter-spell and neither side could gain any advantage. Next the warriors of each side fought a bitter, pitched battle. Both armies lost many of their men but at last the Children of Nemed were victorious and the Fomorians were overcome. Conann, however, was still safe inside his tower so next the Children of Nemed let loose the wolves and poisonous pigs they had brought with them. Most of the people who were inside fled from this fearsome attack but still Conann refused to leave. Finally, Fergus, the son of Nemed, challenged Conann to meet him in single combat and after a fierce fight, Conann was killed.

The struggle was not over yet, however, for a new contingent of vengeful Fomorians arrived. The Children of Nemed were waiting for them and challenged them as they left their ships; once again fierce fights broke out. So carried away were they by the heat and the fury and the noise of the battle that no-one observed a huge wave racing towards them. Higher than the tower itself and faster than any hawk, its huge form was accompanied by a terrible roar as if from some gigantic beast of the sea. As it crashed onto the beach, it broke over the people fighting there, overwhelming them all so that only thirty of the Children of Nemed and a boatload of Fomorians survived.

After this disaster, the Children of Nemed were never able to settle down again. They lived in constant fear of the Fomorians and of the plague, and they argued and disagreed amongst themselves continually. Eventually they went away, some back to Greece, others to make their home in Britain; Ireland was left uninhabited except for the wild Fomorians for some two hundred years.

The conquest by the Fir Bolg

The second invasion was by a people called the Fir Bolg. They were descended from those Children of Nemed who had returned to settle in Greece and in time grown into a powerful tribe again. As they grew stronger, the Greeks became afraid of them and made them work as slaves to keep them under control. They were forced to turn rough, stony places into plains sweet with clover, carrying all the soil from far away so that the plants could grow. It was gruelling work which broke their spirits and exhausted their strength. Finally, they held a counsel and decided to escape. They sewed curraghs (coracles) out of skins, making them more seaworthy with the hempen sacks they used for transporting soil. Then they set out for Ireland, their own land, the home of their ancestors.

The Fir Bolg were the first invaders to establish social and political order in the land. When they arrived in Ireland, they divided the country into five provinces which are still there today: Ulster, Leinster, Munster, Connacht and finally Meath, the centre of the country. They also introduced the custom of kingship, obeying the rule of a king whom they considered as semi-divine, instead of the warlords of the past; and they lived in Ireland in fruitful prosperity for many generations.

The conquest by the gods

The third group to invade the land of Ireland was perhaps the most mysterious and important of all. According to Celtic tradition, the Tuatha De Danann, the Children of Danu, are the gods of Ireland, although the earlier invaders clearly also had divine characteristics and functions. It is the Tuatha De who are remembered by the people today as the gods and their deeds and cult legends are commemorated; there is little doubt that they are, in fact, the old gods of the Celts and that their stories reflect the beliefs not only of the ancient Irish but of a great part of prehistoric Europe.

The Tuatha De Danann were the direct descendants of Nemed, through his grandson, who had left Ireland with his family and had settled in the northern islands of Greece. There his people had increased greatly and it was there that they learned all the arts of druidism and magic, in which they became very skilled. They fought on the side of the Athenians against the Philistines and astonished everyone by their marvellous feats, using their druidic arts to gain victories for the Athenians. At last the Philistines became so dangerous that the Tuatha De Danann had to flee from Greece and find

another homeland. Like their ancestors, they sailed away to the west, carrying with them their most treasured possessions. Among these were four sacred objects which appear again and again throughout the Celtic myths: the Lia Fail, a stone which uttered a shriek at the inauguration of a rightful king; the invincible spear of Lugh; the deadly sword of Nuada; and the ever-plentiful cauldron of the Dagda, the 'Good god', the father-god of Ireland.

First, they took refuge in Scotland but the country was bleak and the life of the exiles harsh so that very soon the Tuatha De decided to attack Ireland, which they believed rightfully belonged to them.

This army of the gods landed on the shores of Ireland in secret at the festival of Beltain (1 May), the most sacred of all the Celtic feasts. When everyone had come ashore, they burned all their boats so they could not run away if the Fir Bolg, who now ruled Ireland, should prove too formidable. Then they conjured up a magical darkness all around themselves to help them move about the country unperceived and soon, at a place called Connacht, they surprised the Fir Bolg.

Fearful battles were fought before the Fir Bolg were forced to admit defeat. Those who were not slain fled to remote islands around the coasts and there they continued to live. The troubles of the Tuatha De were not over, however, for the wild Fomorians ranged their evil forces against them and it was not until after the great battle known as the Second Battle of Moytura that they were finally overcome. The story of that mighty encounter of good and evil is told in the next chapter.

The conquest by the Sons of Mil

The fourth great invasion of Ireland was made by people from Spain. While the invasion of the Tuatha De is the most important for Celtic mythology, that of the Sons of Mil is the most important for Celtic history, for this was the coming of the Gaels to Ireland, and they have been there ever since. Possessed of magical qualities themselves, through the powers of the druids, their battle against the gods represents man's eternal fight against supernatural forces. Some of the characters, such as Donn, appear throughout the wider Celtic world. There is, for example, Donnotaurus or 'Lordly bull' in Gaul. In other tales Donn figures as the god of death, to whose house all who die are invited.

Emer, Donn and Eremon were the sons of Mil of Spain. Their uncle, a man of great magic powers and learning had seen Ireland in a vision and travelled there, only to be treacherously killed by the Tuatha De. When the news reached the Sons of Mil they quickly decided what to do. They knew that Ireland was a land of good grain and grazing, with fine honey, plentiful fish in the rivers, lakes and seas and that it had a pleasant climate; bent on invasion and revenge, they gathered together their families and goods and set sail. Donn, the oldest son, was the leader of a fleet of sixty-five ships and forty chieftains; their spiritual leader was a man named Amergin, a poet skilled in all the arts of magic.

As the fleet approached Ireland and prepared to land, the Tuatha De used druidic magic to

make the whole country disappear. The sailors
stared speechlessly, seeing only open sea where
a moment before there had been rocky shores
and thickly forested hills but Amergin realized
at once that supernatural forces were at work.
He advised Donn to sail three times around the
vanished island and when this was done, the
spell was broken, the coastlands reappeared as
miraculously as they had vanished, and the Sons
of Mil landed at Inber Scene in the south-west
of Ireland on the eve of Beltain.

As they marched inland, they met in turn the
three goddesses of Ireland: Banba, Fodla and
finally Eriu after whom as Erin the land is still
named. These three were the ancient territorial
deities and it was very important for the invaders
to obtain their co-operation. The first two
goddesses said little but Eriu was fulsome in her
praise and told them that their arrival had long

been prophesied and that they were expected. 'You are welcome to this place, for this is the best island in the world and yours the most perfect race: you are destined to rule here for ever.'

'If that is true,' Donn replied 'it will be due not to your help but to the power of our gods and fighting men.'

Angry at this arrogant answer, Eriu foretold that Donn and his descendants would never rule in Ireland but that his line would be cursed for ever.

Leaving Eriu, the Sons of Mil advanced to Tara, seat of kings and the chief sanctuary of ancient Ireland. There they found the three husbands of the goddesses, the three kings of the Tuatha De: Mac Cuill (Son of Hazel), Mac Cecht (Son of Plough) and Mac Greine (Son of Sun). These three sneered at the sons of Mil for trying to take Ireland by surprise, for they considered this a dishonourable act. They gave the foreigners the choice of leaving Ireland, submitting to the Tuatha De or fighting. Donn was spoiling for a fight but the druid Amergin had ultimate authority in this matter.

'Let them keep the land until we come a second time to take it from them openly,' he commanded.

'Where shall we go then?' asked Donn.

'Way out beyond the ninth wave,' replied the Amergin, speaking in the magical words of the druids.

'If you take my advice,' persisted Donn, 'it will be war.' But the Sons of Mil obeyed Amergin and set sail again until they were nine waves distance from the land.

'Now,' said the Tuatha De, 'we must make sure that they never get back to Ireland.' Using their magic powers, they called up druidic winds and a terrifying storm. The massive waves were so violent that even the gravel from the sea bed was lifted up to the top of the waves, and there was great confusion and terror among the sailors as their ships were driven helplessly westwards out into the open sea.

'This is no natural storm but a druid's wind,' cried Donn above the sound of the waves.

'We cannot be certain until we know how high in the air it blows,' replied Amergin. 'If it blows no higher than the mast, it is druids' work.'

One of the men climbed the violently swaying mast and stretched his hand into the air above; it was quite calm and still but as he leaned down to call to the men below a sudden gust of wind tore him from the mast and he fell to his death on the deck far beneath him.

Then Amergin stood up in the bows and chanted a magic poem to appease the goddess Eriu whom Donn had offended and at once a great calm came in place of the storm.

Donn, however was still full of pride. 'If only I could get ashore I would put all the warriors of Ireland to the spear and the sword,' he declared and this arrogance and disobedience to Amergin sealed his fate. Once more the storm howled around them and the waves were wilder than ever. In the noise, confusion and terror of the raging seas, Donn's ship became parted from the others and, as Donn defied the elements with his sword, was wrecked off the south-west coast. Donn and all his men were drowned.

The rest of the fleet was divided under the command of Emer and Eremon, the two remaining brothers, and landed once more on the shore. As Amergin, miraculously saved from the waves, set his right foot on the sand, he uttered a powerful poem, claiming the land and all it contained for himself and for the Sons of Mil.

The invaders had outwitted the magic of the Tuatha De but there were many battles to be fought before they could claim final victory. Even when the Tuatha De had been defeated in battle, they still retained all their magic powers and supernatural skills and they made life so difficult for the newcomers that eventually a truce was made between the two forces.

It was agreed to divide the country between them, the territory underground to belong to the Tuatha De and the land above it to the Sons of Mil. As a result, the Tuatha De went to live underground. The Dagda gave a *sidh* or fairy mound to each of their chieftains and ever afterwards these mounds were to be the dwellings of the fairy folk of Ireland. And that was the agreement between the Tuatha De and the Gaels forever.

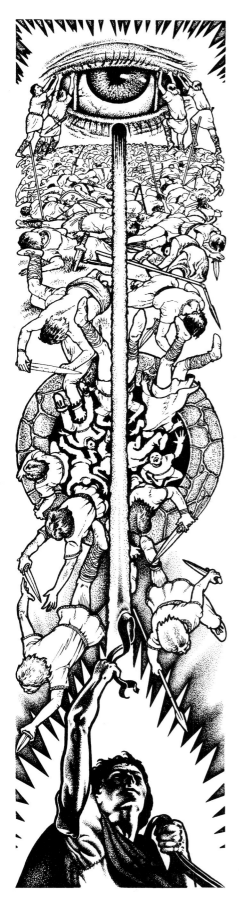

The second battle of Moytura

The story of the second battle of Moytura is one of the most important of the Irish mythological tales. It is set in the time before the coming of the Gaels, when the Tuatha De Danann were fighting for the right to rule in Ireland. When the tale begins, the Tuatha De had defeated the armies of the Fir Bolg and held an uneasy truce with the fierce tribes of the Fomorians.

The Tuatha De were led by Nuada, their king. Among them were Ogma, renowned for his strength and eloquence; Diancecht the physician and god of medicine with his sons Cian, Cu, Cethan and Miach and his daughter Airmid; Goibniu the smith; Luchta the carpenter and Credne the metalworker. The Dagda, the 'good god', was the father-god of them all. Another important person makes his first appearance in this story, a young man named Lugh Long Arm, who appears in the mythology of the Celtic world as both a great warrior and a shining god of the sun.

The sinister Fomorians, too, had their more than human heroes and champions including Balor, King of the Isles, who, like the leaders of the Tuatha De, was both warrior and god. The conflict between these two powerful forces is indeed a battle of the gods.

In the final battle between the Tuatha De and the Fir Bolg (known as the first battle of Moytura) the king of the Fir Bolg was slain and Nuada himself was terribly wounded when his arm was hacked right off at the shoulder. He survived this fearful blow and Diancecht the physican made him a silver arm to replace the one he had lost; but according to the law of the Tuatha De, a king must be whole and unblemished and Nuada Silver Arm could no longer be their ruler. The man who was chosen to rule the newly conquered land was Eochaid Bres, or Eochaid the Beautiful, the son of a woman named Elotha. His father was not one of the Tuatha De but a chief of the Fomorians. Bres, however, knew nothing of his father and was brought up by his mother's people. He lived up to his name, being as beautiful as he was brave and strong and when he was chosen as king, a marriage was arranged between him and Tailltiu, the widow of the dead king of the Fir Bolg. Another marriage, this time between a Fomorian and one of the Tuatha De, was celebrated at the same time for Cian, the son of Diancecht the physician, married Ethne, daughter of the great warrior Balor, King of the Isles.

Bres was made king only on condition that he would abdicate if his reign no longer pleased the people but he had not been king for long before he began to favour the wild Fomorian people over the Tuatha De. The Fomorians incited him to oppress the Tuatha De, and he began to force them to pay tribute and to perform difficult and often menial tasks. Eventually the Tuatha De rebelled and called upon Bres to remember the conditions on which he had been made king and to renounce the kingship. Angrily, Bres had to agree but he begged to be allowed to remain for seven years and this request was granted.

Bres had asked for this respite so that he might gather together the warriors of the Fomorians and smash the tribes of the Tuatha De who had rejected him. Now at last he learned who he really was for his mother took him to the Fomorians' lands and there the chieftain who was his father acknowledged him as his son. Then his father sent him to the great warrior Balor, King of the Isles and to Indech, King of the Fomorians, and they gathered together all their forces to make a large and fearsome army. It was said that they were so numerous they formed a living bridge from the western isles of Scotland all the way to Ireland.

At the time when the Tuatha De had decided the oppression of Bres was too much to bear, Nuada Silver Arm was miraculously healed. It happened like this. The flesh around the silver arm had begun to fester and Nuada sent for Miach, the son of Diancecht, who was known to have amazing powers of healing. Miach examined the wound, then asked that the long-buried arm should be found and put in place of the silver one. When this was done, he chanted, 'Let this be joined sinew to sinew, and nerve to nerve so that there is movement and feeling in every joint,' and in three days Nuada was completely healed.

Though Nuada was now restored to health and strength, Miach's healing skills had fatal consequences. Diancecht was so jealous of his son's superior powers that he threw his sword at the boy, wounding him in the head. Miach was skilled enough to heal himself easily but

Diancecht struck him a second time, this time wounding him to the bone. Again Miach healed himself. A third blow cut into the brain and the fourth destroyed it so completely that even Miach's powers were defeated. Miach was buried but still his knowledge did not die for 365 healing herbs grew from his grave, one herb for each of his joints and sinews. His sister Airmid picked them carefully and arranged them according to their properties, but Diancecht was again jealous of his son and he mixed them all up so that no-one could tell what each was supposed to do. If he had left them, the cure for every illness would still be known.

Nuada had been reinstated as king of the Tuatha De when his arm was healed and to celebrate the event, he made a splendid feast for his people at Tara. During the celebrations the doorkeeper saw a strange company approaching led by a young, fair, shapely warrior in regal robes.

'Who are you and what is your purpose here?' asked the doorkeeper.

'Tell the king that Lugh Long Arm is here,' replied the stranger, 'the son of Cian, son of Diancecht, and of Ethne, daughter of Balor, and foster-son of Tailltiu. Take me to King Nuada for I can help him.'

'What skill do you practise, for no-one enters Tara without qualifications?' replied the doorkeeper.

'Question me,' said Lugh, 'I am a carpenter.'

'We have no need of you here for we have a carpenter already,' replied the doorkeeper.

'Question me doorkeeper. I am a smith.'

'We have a smith already, Goibniu,' said the doorkeeper, 'we do not need another.'

'I am a champion warrior,' said Lugh.

'We have warriors of our own,' said the doorkeeper, 'and Ogma is our champion.'

'I am a harpist.'

'We have one.'

I am a man skilled in the arts and strategies of war.'

'We have others like you.'

'I am a poet and historian.'

'We have one already.'

'I am a sorcerer.'

'We have sorcerers and druids more powerful than any in the land.'

'I am a physician.'

'Diancecht is our physician.'

'I am a cupbearer.'

'We have plenty.'

'I am a metalworker.'

'Our metalworker is Credne.'

'Then,' said Lugh, 'go and ask the king if he has a man who has all these skills and learning together. If he has I will not enter Tara.'

When he heard this message from the doorkeeper, Nuada sent his best chess-player to test the stranger's mental skills—but Lugh defeated him easily. Then the king invited him into the fortress and gave him the seat reserved for the wisest man, for Lugh had knowledge of every art.

Ogma, the champion of both strength and eloquence, was eager to prove his own strength in front of this stranger and he heaved up one of the palace's huge flagstones. With enormous effort he pushed it through the wall of the royal house so that it landed right outside the fortification. Without a word, Lugh accepted the challenge, picked the stone up easily and threw it back inside, then in an instant repaired the damage it had done to the wall of the royal house.

Recognizing Lugh as a true champion, Nuada made the brilliant, all-skilled youth responsible for the defence of Ireland against the evil Fomorians. He placed Lugh in his own chair and a great conference took place while the Tuatha De decided what course should be taken. Under Lugh's leadership, each man undertook to use his special skills to help in the fight. Diancecht the physician would cure the wounded; Goibniu the smith would repair their broken weapons and Credne the metalworker would provide new swords, shields and lances. Ogma would fight with all his strength and the Dagda would use all his skill to outwit the enemy. Sorcerers and druids, cupbearers and carpenters all agreed to play their parts. Finally it was agreed that Lugh, the Dagda and Ogma should go to the three warrior goddesses and learn from them how the battle should be planned. The Dagda had an arrangement to meet one of the goddesses, the Morrigan, every year at Samain (Hallowe'en) and when the time came he persuaded her to reveal the Fomorians' plans and fight on the side of the Tuatha De.

So all was arranged and it took to the end of seven years to make the preparations and forge the weapons.

The Tuatha De were still not completely ready for war, however, so the Dagda went to the Fomorians to seek a truce and so gain more time. The Fomorians invited him in and urged him to eat with them. Knowing that the Dagda was a glutton for porridge, they prepared a huge cauldron of oatmeal and threw into it whole carcasses of goats, cattle and sheep. When it was all well mixed and cooked, the Fomorians dug a cauldron-sized pit and poured the porridge into it, threatening the Dagda with death unless he could consume every scrap of that giant meal. 'For we do not wish to be accused of inhospitality,' they said solemnly.

Undaunted, the Dagda seized his ladle, which was big enough for a man and a woman to lie in, and ate up all the porridge, scraping the bottom of the pit with his finger to get up the very last scraps. After his vast meal, his belly itself was bigger than a cauldron and he fell asleep while the Fomorians laughed at him. When he stood up to go he could hardly walk and he staggered off, his great stomach adding to his extremely uncouth appearance. His short cape and brown tunic only reached to his buttocks and his brogues were made of horse hide with the hairy side out. He used as a weapon a wheeled club which it would have taken eight strong men to carry and the track that it made as he leaned his great weight on it was so deep and so enduring that it served as a boundary dyke for the province and for that reason was ever after called 'The Track of the Dagda's Club'.

The Fomorians laughed and mocked him until he was out of sight—but the Dagda had won the time the Tuatha De needed for their preparations and he returned content to Tara.

The Tuatha De had resolved that Lugh was too valuable to risk his life in battle so when the army assembled, he was placed under the guard of nine of his warriors, in charge of the strategy but not allowed to fight against the enemy.

The rival armies faced each other finally on the eve of Samain and the battle began with noise, shouting and the clanging of shields. For several days the battle raged, with champions from each side meeting in single combat. Sometimes one of the Tuatha De was victorious, sometimes a Fomorian but the Fomorians soon noticed that they were at a disadvantage: unlike their own casualties, the wounded and even the dead of the Tuatha De were always alive and fit for battle again the next day, their broken weapons mended, their battered shields as good as new.

The Fomorians sent a spy, Ruadan, to find out how this was possible and, disguised as one of the Tuatha De, he made his way to the enemy camp. He soon discovered that Goibniu the smith, Luchta the carpenter and Credne the metalworker had formed a powerful, magical team and were rapidly mending the weapons as soon as they were broken. And he saw how Diancecht the physician and his sons cast spells over a healing well: when the dead and wounded were thrown into its waters they were instantly healed or restored to life.

Angrily, Ruadan attacked Goibniu in his forge and wounded him with his spear; but Goibniu plucked the spear from his body and threw it back at Ruadan, sending him staggering back to die among his people. His mission did not fail completely, however, for with his last breath he told the Fomorians about the well and they came and filled it in with stones.

Until now, the battle had been fought between individual champions but now the two armies drew their forces together for a pitched battle. As they confronted each other, the Fomorians suddenly saw a shining figure driving his chariot in the forefront of the Tuatha De. Lugh had escaped from his guards and was there among his fighters, standing on tiptoe so that all could see him and urging them on to victory.

The battle was fast and furious and the carnage terrible as men and warrior women on both sides were struck down. Then Balor, King of the Isles, killed Nuada Silver Arm and Lugh fought his way through the throng to confront the man who was his own grandfather.

Balor was known as Balor Evil Eye because one of his eyes had special magic powers. Once, when his father's druids had been brewing spells outside his house, Balor had looked out of the window. The fumes from the brew had wafted into his eye and the poison from the charms had entered it. So powerful were the spells that one glance from the poisonous eye would destroy an army and so it was only opened on the battlefield. As Lugh came face to face with his grandfather he shouted a fierce challenge.

'Lift up my eyelid,' commanded Balor, 'so that I may see this chatterer.'

Four men holding a strong wooden peg were needed to lift the heavy lid and before it was half raised on the evil eye, Lugh cast a stone from his sling. The stone passed straight through the eye and carried it out through the back of Balor's head where its gaze destroyed twenty-seven Fomorians who were nearby. With Balor dead, the Tuatha De fought with renewed ferocity and, urged on by the Morrigan and the other war goddesses, they drove the Fomorians into the sea. Bres fled with them. When the battle was quite over, the slain were as numerous on the battlefield as the stars in the heavens or the flakes of snow in a blizzard. Some say that the great standing stones on the plain of Carrowmore near Sligo still mark the graves where the dead of the second battle of Moytura lie.

At last the land was free of the Fomorians and the Tuatha De were restored to their former positions. Only then did the Morrigan, the war goddess of Ireland, climb to the mountain tops to chant a paeon of victory to the royal land and to the fairy hosts of Ireland.

The sorrows of storytelling

The group of stories known as 'The three sorrows of storytelling' was written down in late medieval times but their themes are much older than that. The two given here are both concerned with characters belonging to the Tuatha De. The first, 'The Fate of the children of Tuirenn', is a very ancient mythological story of shape-changing, magic and revenge.

Cian the Mighty, the father of Lugh Long Arm, was one of the three surviving sons of Diancecht the physician. He and his two brothers Cu and Cethen were sworn enemies of three other brothers, the three sons of Tuirenn, named Brian, Iuchar and Iuchabar. The two families could not meet without quarrelling and were always eager to fight one another if given the slightest provocation.

In the days when the Tuatha De were still threatened by the Fomorians, Lugh came to his father and his two uncles one day to seek their help against an expected invasion. The three brothers agreed to come at once and separated to spread news of the attack around the country. Cian went northwards to the Plain of Mag Murthemne and there to his dismay he saw the three sons of Tuirenn walking towards him in full battle array, for they too were on their way to the fight. Knowing that alone he was no match for the three of them, he looked around for a way of escape. Nearby he saw a large herd of swine so in an instant he struck himself with his magical druidic wand, changed himself into a pig and began to root about among the grasses with the rest of the herd.

The three brothers had all spotted Cian and when he suddenly disappeared from view, Brian asked the others where he had gone. 'We do not know,' they replied.
'Cowards,' said Brian. 'You should keep a better watch on things. The warrior has struck himself with a wand of gold and turned himself into one of those pigs over there.'
'That's bad,' said his brothers, 'for the pigs belong to one of the Tuatha De and even if we kill them all, the druidic pig may still escape.'
'You've learned your lessons badly if you can't tell a druidic pig from a real one,' said Brian and he instantly struck them both with a

25

druidic stick and transformed them into a pair
of hounds. Off they went, howling, on the trail
of the druidic pig which soon separated from
the others and made for a grove of trees. Just
before it entered the grove, however, Brian cast
his spear through its chest. The pig screamed at
them: 'You have done an evil thing.'
'I see you speak in human language,' said Brian.
'Until today I was in human form,' replied the
druidic pig. 'I am Cian, son of Diancecht. Give
me quarter.'
'Indeed and we are sorry for what has happened
to you,' said Iuchar and Iucharba, who had
resumed their human forms. But Brian said, 'I
swear by my gods of the air that if life were to
return to you seven times over I should deprive
you of it.'
'Well,' said Cian, 'grant me one request. Let me
regain my own form.'
'That you may,' said Brian, 'for I often feel it
less distasteful to kill a man than a pig.'
    Then Cian took on his own shape again and
said, 'You must give me quarter fit for a man
now.'
'That we shall not give you,' said Brian.
'Well I have tricked you anyway,' retorted
Cian, 'for if you had slain me in the form of a

pig you could have only been fined for the worth of the pig. But as I am to be slain in my own form, a nobleman, there never has been and never will be a greater honour-price to pay than that which you will pay for my death. My son is Lugh and he will know by the marks of your weapons by whom I was slain.'
'Then we shall not use weapons but rocks' said Brian and he picked up a heavy stone and hurled it at Cian's head. Soon Cian lay dead and when the brothers had buried his broken body, they continued on their way to fight the Fomorians.

Lugh led the armies and a great battle was fought and won. When it was over, he asked if anyone had seen his father in the battle and when he was told no, he knew that he was dead. 'He lives not,' said Lugh, 'and by my word I shall neither eat nor drink until I discover the manner by which my father died.'

So Lugh and his men set off and searched the land until they came to the place where Cian had died. And there the ground itself spoke: 'Your father was in great peril here, O Lugh, for when he saw the children of Tuirenn he was alone and was forced to transform himself into a pig. But it was in his own form that they killed him.'

Lugh ordered the men to dig up the body so that he might know how his father had been killed. The terrible nature of Cian's wounds filled him with grief and anger.

After Lugh had chanted a long mourning lay, Cian was reburied with all ceremony. A tombstone was raised over his grave, with his name written in Ogam, the ancient Celtic script, and the funeral games were held.

Then Lugh went to Tara and sat next to the king and there he saw the three sons of Tuirenn, beautiful, skilled and much-loved. Lugh stood up in front of the people and called for silence. 'Children of the goddess Danu,' he said, 'what penalty should a man demand from those who have murdered his father?'

The assembled people looked at one another in amazement, not knowing what he meant. 'Cian is dead,' said Lugh, 'and his murderers are here in your midst.'
'The men who did this terrible thing deserve to die themselves,' said the king and the people,

including the three guilty brothers, murmured their approval. 'But if I were the murderer I would ask you to accept an honour-price rather than take my life,' he continued.

Then Brian, the oldest of the sons of Tuirenn stood up and confessed to the murder of Cian, and Lugh agreed to accept a fine rather than to take their lives.
'This is your punishment,' said Lugh. 'You shall obtain three apples and the skin of a pig, and a spear, and two horses and a chariot, seven pigs, a puppy, a cooking spit and three shouts upon a hill: that is the compensation I demand.'

The sons of Tuirenn were surprised at the smallness of the penalty but afraid that they were being tricked, for they knew Lugh's powers and his fury. It was not until they had sworn their agreement in the presence of the king and all the nobles of Ireland that Lugh explained the impossibility of the task.
'The three apples are the apples from the Garden of the Hesperides. Whoever eats them is cured of all wounds and disease without diminishing them in any way. And whoever throws one hits anything he wishes without losing the apple he casts. They are guarded day and night and no man can obtain them.'
'The pig-skin belongs to the King of Greece. It too has healing powers; and water passed through it turns nine days later to wine.'
'The spear is the poisoned spear of the King of Persia and the two horses and chariot belong to the King of Sicily and can run over land and sea wherever their driver directs. The seven pigs are no ordinary pigs, either. They are those of the King of the Golden Pillars and though they are killed every night, yet next day they are alive again as ever.'
'The puppy you must obtain from the King of Ioruaidhe for she can catch every wild animal she sees. And the cooking spit lies at the bottom of the sea between Britain and Erin.'
'You have promised finally to give three shouts upon a hill, but I require them to be given on the hill where Miodhchaoin, who taught my father the arts of war, lives with his sons. He will not forgive your shameful deeds and you will fail in this task as in the others.'

Silent and dismayed, the three brothers set

The Children of Lir

This story is not as old as the story of the children of Tuirenn but its theme connects it with the earliest stories of Irish mythology. It is set in the time after the conquest of the Gaels, when the Tuatha De had taken to the *sidh* mounds of their underground kingdom. Lir, the father of Manannan the sea-god, is the same character used by Shakespeare in his play 'King Lear'.

Once, when the kingship of the Tuatha De fell vacant an election was held to choose the next king. Bobd Deargh was chosen and Lir, who lived in the *sidh* at Fionnachaidh in northern Ireland, was offended since he had hoped to be made king himself. He left the assembly without taking his leave of anyone and retired to the north in a rage.

Some time later Lir's beloved wife died and he fell into a wasting-sickness and could not be consoled. Bodb saw his chance to be reconciled with Lir and he offered him one of his three foster-daughters to be his wife. In those days all noble children were sent away from home to be brought up in different aristocratic households and foster sons and daughters were as close to one another and to their foster parents as blood relations.

Lir chose Aeb, the oldest foster-daughter and took her back to his *sidh*, where a great wedding feast was held. In due course she bore him twins: a son, Aed, and a daughter, Fionnguala. Soon she became pregnant once more, and again gave birth to twins, two boys, Fiachra and Conn; but the birth cost her her life. Lir was again stricken with grief and only his children could bring him any comfort. Bodb then offered Lir a second foster-daughter, Aoife, as his wife, and Lir took her home to his *sidh* in the north. At first Aoife worshipped her sister's children and did all that she could for them. Bodb, too, loved them like his own grandchildren and they often went to visit him at his royal dwelling. The four children delighted and entertained everyone and their father doted on them.

However, before long Aoife became deeply jealous of their popularity and she pretended to

out on their task, leaving the shores of Ireland far behind.

The long years passed and against all odds, the children of Tuirenn accomplished all their daunting tasks. The last, however, brought them near to death for the fight with Miodhchaoin and his sons was hard and left them badly wounded. Only Lugh had the power to heal their deadly wounds but when Brian begged him to cure them he refused. 'If you were to give me the breadth of the earth in solid gold I would not save you, for the dreadful death you gave my beloved father.'

So Brian returned to his two brothers and lay down beside them and they died. Their father came to them and mourned, for he loved them. Then he, too, fell dead beside them and the four were buried together in the same grave.

And that was the tragic fate of the children of Tuirenn, killed by the force of Lugh's revenge.

be ill. She lay on her couch for nearly a year, planning how she could destroy her step-children. Finally, having decided upon a treacherous scheme, she rose, apparently recovered from her long sickness, and prepared to take the children on a visit to Bodb.

Fionnguala, the girl twin, had a premonition of evil and was unwilling to accompany her step-mother, but she could not avoid her fate and they set out for their grandfather's house. When they had travelled some distance Aoife turned to her attendants and servants and said fiercely, 'Kill Lir's children for they have deprived me of their father's love. Ask any reward of me and you shall have it.'
'No,' they replied angrily, 'we cannot kill them. It is evil enough even to contemplate such a deed and to speak of it is utterly wicked.' Aoife then considered killing them herself with her sword—for women were warriors in those days and carried swords and daggers—but she had not the courage to carry it out.

They travelled on until they came to Lake Derryvaragh in West Meath, and there she commanded the children to bathe in the lake. No sooner had they entered the water than she turned them into swans with her druidic wand.

Sadly, the swan maiden Fionnguala called out to Aoife, accusing her and prophesying her destruction.
'Since you have cursed us with this transformation, let there at least be a time when its power will cease,' pleaded Fionnguala.
'For three hundred years you must live on Derryvaragh, for three hundred years in Scotland and for three hundred years in Erris and Inishglory. But when a man from Connacht in the north shall be united with a woman from Munster in the south, then you shall be released,' replied Aoife triumphantly. She knew that because the children themselves had requested her to fix the length of their enchantment, there was no power left to the Tuatha De to lift the curse. Even Aoife could not undo the curse and, afraid of her husband's anger, she granted the swans certain qualities not possessed by ordinary birds: the power of eloquence and the gift of singing which would be unrivalled by any music in the world. They would also retain their human senses and faculties but they would not suffer distress because they were in swan-form.

Aoife continued her journey to Bodb's palace and when he asked her where his grandchildren were, she replied that Lir would not trust him with them any longer. Enraged, Bodb sent his messengers to Lir and so Aoife's treachery was revealed. At once Bodb seized his druidic rod and struck her down, turning her into a demon and as such she is condemned to wander through the air for ever.

Then Bodb and Lir went down to the lake together and there they saw the four most lovely swans the world has ever seen. As they stood there, the birds began to sing their sweet, magic music and all the pain and sorrow, the rage and the despair fell from everyone who heard it.

For three hundred years, all the people of Ireland flocked to the shores of Lake Derryvaragh to see the druidic swans. During the day, the swans conversed with them, for they had the gift of eloquence, of poetry, and of fine speech. In the night they raised their heavenly voices and sang the whole company to sleep. And no matter how sick they were, no matter what weight of worldly cares lay upon them, whoever heard them slept a calm and care-less sleep to the wild sweet singing of the children of Lir.

After three hundred years, Fionnguala, the leader of the swans, told her brothers that they must leave their beloved lake. As she chanted a poem of sad farewell, the four swans encircled the waters of the lake three times, then winged their sorrowful way to their bleak exile in Scotland. There, in sorrow and loneliness, they endured many hardships. On one storm-tossed night they were driven apart by the fierce winds. All night long Fionnguala waited on Seal Rock and in the morning she saw Conn coming towards her, bedraggled and exhausted. Next came Fiachra, chilled and weakened, and Fionnguala took both her brothers under her loving wings, saying,
'Now, if only Aed would come to us we would lament no more.' At last he too appeared, hardly able to fly, and so the four poor

creatures were united once more.

One day they were swimming in the estuary of the River Bann when they saw a party of horsemen approaching. It was Bodb's two sons, with a great host of people from the Otherworld who had been searching for them far and wide. They gave the swans news of their people, the Tuatha De, and told them that Lir and Bodb were well and happy, except for their lasting sorrow at the absence of Lir's children.

With a bursting heart Fionnguala lamented their grim fate.
'The dwelling place of the noble children of Lir is cold and comfortless. They now wear feathers in place of silk. The fruits of the white sands and the salty sea are their food instead of the mead of the hazel tree.'

Three hundred years passed and it was time to go to Erris and Inishglory. There they remained, in exile and suffering, until Saint Patrick came to bring Christianity to Ireland and Saint Mo Chaemoc built his little oratory on Inishglory.

One morning after the bell for matins had been rung and the singing of the monks was finished, the swans lifted up their own unearthly voices and sang with passion their most marvellous melodies. Mo Chaemoc, who had not heard the story of the enchanted swans, enquired where the wonderful music came from and when the people told him, he called the swans to him and joined Fionnguala to Aed and Conn to Fiachra with silver chains, as a sign that they were under enchantment and that he knew them to be of human origin.

The swans remained there to the constant delight of the saint and in his company all their own suffering was forgotten. Then at last the time came when Aoife's ancient prophesy was fulfilled and Lairgrin, now king of Connacht, married Deoch, the daughter of the king of Munster. Deoch soon learned of the famous swans of Inishglory and, coveting them for herself, she sent servants to take them from Mo Chaemoc by force. And so the prophesy was fulfilled: violence broke the long enchantment and instead of singing swans, the servants saw before them four ancient, wizened mortals.

Then Mo Chaemoc baptized them and they died and ascended into the Christian heaven to find peace at last; but the saint Mo Chaemoc mourned the loss of his beloved swans.

The story of Cu Chulainn

The collection of stories known as the Ulster Cycle dates from between 100 BC to AD 100, around the beginning of the Christian era. It is set in Ulster in the reign of Conchobar mac Nessa and the central figure is Cu Chulainn, the greatest of all Irish heroes.

The most important part of the cycle is the sequence 'The Cattle Raid of Cooley' (*Tain Bo Cuailnge*) which is the oldest epic in western European literature. In length, in literary quality and in drama, it equals the Iliad and the Odyssey of Bronze Age Greece. Connected to it are several minor tales that add detail and background to the main story.

The Greek tales are dead. The remarkable thing about the *Tain* and the stories linked to it is that they are alive today in the folk memory and oral tradition of the Gaels of Ireland and Scotland, having survived the long centuries of disruption and the disintegration of Celtic tribal society. The world of the *Tain* is crude and primitive but not barbaric. There are strict codes of behaviour and a strong sense of the 'fitness' of things. There is much humour and a great deal of pathos. Its values go back to an early common Indo-European world and it mirrors an essentially tribal Iron Age society in which wealth was largely measured in terms of cattle, and cattle-raiding was a favourite occupation.

The epic as recorded in early Irish is stark and swift yet often moving, and at times beautiful. A sense of country is always present and it is firmly set in territories which we can still traverse today. It is still possible to walk the hills and pace the plains, and follow in the footsteps—or chariot wheels—of the men of Connacht and of Ulster, with their charioteers, their foot soldiers, their druids and poets, and their great, raging, semi-human bulls, for mythology also plays a strong part in this raucous tale. The human dilemma of conflicting loyalties is also always to the fore.

The *Tain Bo Cuailnge* is one of the great jewels of the early, native literature of the British Isles, sadly a much neglected heritage.

We begin the story some time before the birth of Christ, when a famous king named Conchobar mac Nessa ruled in Emain Macha, the great royal stronghold of Ulster. His reign was good, and this was reflected in the prosperity of his people. The cattle grew fat in the rich pasture lands and the sweet hill-grazings. The harvests were rich in grain and in fruits of every kind, and the seas, the rivers and the lakes were full of excellent fish.

Dechtire was one of the king's sisters, and for three years she mysteriously vanished from Emain Macha with fifty of her handmaids. When she returned, she brought with her a baby son named Setanta who had been born in mysterious circumstances. He was the son of Lugh Long Arm of the Tuatha De, the great god of the Otherworld.

Setanta was reared by his step-father and his mother, Dechtire, in their great oaken house on the Plain of Murthemne. He grew quickly and by the time he was six, he was as strong and agile as a boy twice his age. It was then that he heard about the great game of shinty that was played at the court of Conchobar mac Nessa. One hundred and fifty boys were involved in the game and the king himself took a great interest since these were to be his future warriors.

The little boy pestered his mother to let him go and join the game but she was afraid for him and told him he must stay at home until he was older.

'Tell me then, mother,' begged Setanta, 'in what direction does Emain lie?'

'Away to the north,' she answered unthinkingly, 'and it's a rough road that leads there.'

'That doesn't matter,' the boy thought to himself. 'I'll have a go anyway.' So he made himself a toy shield and a toy spear from sticks of wood and taking his shinty stick and ball, he set off for Emain Macha.

Now in those days, before you joined a band of boys playing shinty, you had to approach them and put yourself under their protection for play was hard and fierce. Setanta did not know this and as soon as he reached the field where they game was being played, he walked boldly out and joined in.

'Strange,' said one, 'this lad is clearly from Ulster and yet he insults us.' And they shouted a rough warning to the little boy. When he took no notice, but still ran towards them, they cast their 150 spears at him: he stopped them easily

with his toy shield. Then they flung their shinty balls and sticks at him but he dodged them all.

This apparently unprovoked attack angered Setanta and his whole face and body began to change. His hair stood straight on end and every lock of it seemed to be alight. One of his eyes shrunk to a mere slit while the other grew enormous, as big as a drinking-cup. He drew back his lips to his ears, baring his white teeth and revealing his throat. A halo of fire seemed to rise from his head. Then he charged at the boys and with superhuman force brought down fifty of them before they could escape from the field.

Conchobar was playing chess when he heard the clamour and shouts of what sounded like a major battle and went out to see what was happening.

'That's rough treatment for our lads,' he shouted angrily.

'I am in the right, father Conchobar,' Setanta said. 'I left my home to come and play with them and they were rough to me.'

'Whose son are you?' asked Conchobar.

'I am your nephew Setanta, son of your sister Dechtire, and I certainly did not expect rough treatment here.'

'Well you should have put yourself under the lads' protection,' replied the king.

'I knew nothing about that, but I ask your protection now,' said Setanta.

'You have it,' said the king, and Setanta raced off after the boys.

'What are you going to do to them now?' Conchobar shouted after him.

'Offer them protection from me!' called Setanta.

Setanta made his peace with the other boys and remained in the court and began to learn the arts of war. Some weeks later, Culann the Smith was preparing to entertain the king. He had asked Conchobar not to bring too big a crowd with him as he had not much land or property, only what he could earn by his craft. So when Conchobar set out he took only his finest warriors and fifty chariots with him. As he left, he saw Setanta out on the playing field as usual, beating the other 150 boys single handed. Pleased with the boy's strength and courage, he called him over.

'Come on,' he said, 'I'm taking you to Culann's feast.'

'But I haven't finished my game yet, uncle Conchobar,' said Setanta. 'I'll follow on later.'

Conchobar arrived with his men at Culann's house and as they were about to begin feasting, Culann asked: 'Is there anyone still to come?'

'No,' the king replied, quite forgetting the boy on the shinty pitch.

'I have a vicious hound, who guards my cattle and my household,' explained Culann. 'It takes three men holding his three chains to restrain him.' Then he turned to his servants. 'Unleash the hound and close the gates.'

Towards the end of the afternoon, Setanta came in sight of the stronghold, still hitting his shinty ball with his stick. He took no notice of the snarling dog and walked towards it, still playing. It was only when the men inside heard the dog barking that Conchobar suddenly remembered his nephew. No-one could move: they were sure the boy was doomed. Outside, the huge dog tensed itself to spring but before it leaped on him, Setanta threw his shinty ball into its mouth with such force that it passed right through the dog's body and came out the other end. The dog lay dead at his feet and Setanta appeared nonchalantly at the gate.

When all the shouting and cheering had died down, Culann said sadly, 'You are welcome here for your mother's sake, lad, but it was a terrible misfortune that I ever held this feast. My hound was my life and my income, for he guarded me and all that I have. My best friend has been destroyed.'

'Is there a pup from him?' asked Setanta. 'There is,' replied Culann.

'Then I'll rear him. And until he is fully grown I myself will be your hound. I will not only guard you, I will guard the whole plain of

Murthemne, and not a sheep or a cow will be lost while they are in my charge.'

Then Cathbad the druid, father of the king, spoke. 'Cu Chulainn, Hound of Culann, shall be your name now.'

'I like it,' said Setanta and so he got his name.

A few months later, Cathbad the druid was holding his druidic school at the court. He never had less than a hundred students learning the secrets of druidism and one day one of them asked what the omens for that day were.

'If a warrior takes up arms for the first time this day he will be famous for ever, but his life will be brief,' said Cathbad. Cu Chulainn overheard this and went straight to Conchobar to demand a set of weapons.

'Who told you to ask for weapons?' asked the king.

'Cathbad,' replied the lad and on this authority Conchobar gave him a shield and a spear. They were much too fragile for Cu Chulainn and as soon as he tried them out, they broke like toys. So did all the other weapons that were kept in the royal house for warriors at their initiation. Only the king's own sword and shield withstood Cu Chulainn's strength. He was holding them proudly when Cathbad came in and said, 'It is a pity for so young a boy to be armed.'

'Was it not you who told him to ask for weapons?' asked Conchobar.

'Indeed I did not,' said Cathbad.

Cathbad turned angrily to Cu Chulainn. 'Why did you lie to me, Hound?'

'I did not lie, good Conchobar,' replied Cu Chulainn. 'I heard Cathbad's words this morning.'

Reluctantly Cathbad admitted that the omen must concern Cu Chulainn and when a chariot had been found for him (only the king's was strong enough to hold him) he set out to test his warrior skills.

Cu Chulainn took with him the king's own charioteer, Ibar mac Riangabra, and together they made their way to the border of Ulster. There they met Conall Cearnach whose turn it was to guard the boundary.

'Go back home, Conall,' Cu Chulainn shouted, 'I will guard the boundary today.'

'You could look after poets, lad, but hardly warriors,' Conall said mockingly. It was the last time he made fun of Cu Chulainn for in a moment the boy had smashed the shaft of his chariot and Conall had to return to Emain on foot.

Next Cu Chulainn asked his charioteer Ibar to take him to the top of a high mountain and show him the countryside where he learned the name and size of every fort, surveyed the fields and dwellings and noted the fords and all the secret hiding places. Among the forts was one belonging to three sons who had a blood feud with the Ulstermen. Their father had been killed by one of Conchobar's men and the sons had killed countless warriors in revenge.

'Take me there,' ordered Cu Chulainn.

'Why go in search of danger?' asked Ibar.

'Why avoid it?' Cu Chulainn retorted.

As they drew near to the fort, they stopped to rest in the warm afternoon sun. Just then the three sons rode up.

'Who are you?' they asked threateningly.

'Only a little lad who has taken up arms today,' answered Ibar.

'Then it's bad luck for him,' they said. 'Get out of our territory.'

'I will,' Ibar said, 'but look, the little boy is asleep.'

'I am no ordinary boy,' said Cu Chulainn,

leaping up, 'and I have come here to fight.'
'Good enough,' they said, 'we will meet you in the ford there.'
'Take care,' warned Ibar.
'I swear by the gods of my people,' cried Cu Chulainn, 'that they will slay no more of the men of Ulster.'

One by one the Hound overcame the three brothers, meeting the last in the water of the ford. The river was so deep that water came up to Cu Chulainn's chest but still he managed to strike a mighty blow which struck off the man's head. Carrying the three severed heads, Cu Chulainn and Ibar set off for home.

On the way home Cu Chulainn proved his power over animals as well as over men. As they went, they saw a herd of deer and Cu Chulainn was determined to catch one alive. Leaping from his chariot, he stood in front of the finest animal in the herd and subdued it by the power of his eyes alone. He tied it behind the chariot and they continued on their way. Next he shot at some swans flying overhead with his sling stone and brought them down alive to join the trophies in the chariot. By now the same strange change had come over Cu Chulainn as had happened when he first fought the boys on the shinty field. Full of the frenzy of battle, he drove towards Emain Macha.

Leborcham the poetess looked out from Emain and seeing his furious approach, called out that a terrible warrior was attacking them: 'His face is twisted with rage and in his chariot are the bloody heads of his enemies with a pair of beautiful white birds. A live deer runs behind.'
'I know that one,' said Conchobar, 'it is my sister's son. Let naked women run to him.'

Then all the young women of Emain ran to meet him and Cu Chulainn hid his distorted face from them for shame. Immediately the men seized him and plunged him into three vats of ice-cold water until his battle-fury had left him.

Then Cu Chulainn was restored to his great beauty and they dressed him in a tunic of gold thread, with a green cloak fastened with a silver pin. The lad was placed between the king's knees and Conchobar stroked his hair for he was still only seven years old.

The wooing of Emer

The royal palace at Emain Macha stood on a low hill and was famous for the high rank of its household and the splendour of its banquets. It was a great, circular house, with partitions of bronze and carved pillars of red yew which gave it the name 'House of the Red Branch'. In it were many rooms, the most splendid being that of the king himself. Even when all the warriors of Ulster were gathered there at the same time there was room for everyone. There was always good entertainment in the House of the Red Branch. There were board games such as chess and draughts, the bards sang tales of past glories and chanted poems in praise of the king while the musicians accompanied them on their great Irish harps and lutes. The chariot-warriors displayed their many skills and performed their famous feats of daring, staging mock fights on tight-ropes stretched across the great hall from door to door.

The most daring and skilful of them all was Cu Chulainn and all the women of Emain were sick with love for him. He had marvellous gifts and powers and yet he had three faults which were his youth (for he was beardless so that his enemies mocked him), his reckless daring, and his excessive beauty. His beauty troubled the men of Ulster because all their wives and their daughters were infatuated by him and he was as yet unmarried. His wild daring frightened them for they were afraid that it would bring him to an early death and they loved and needed him.

Eventually they decided that they must find a fitting wife for him, since a man who had a woman of his own would be less likely to ruin their daughters and accept the favours of their wives. Also, if he were to marry and leave an heir, that son would be a re-birth of himself, for the Celts believed in reincarnation.

On the advice of his warriors, Conchobar, the king, tried to find Cu Chulainn a suitable bride, but Cu Chulainn already knew the girl he wanted. This was Emer, the beautiful daughter of a powerful chieftain named Forgall. Emer had all the virtues and qualities required by Cu Chulainn, but, in accordance with the custom of that time, he had to win her by force. He determined to do this without the king's help and so he set out on his quest in his swift chariot, dressed in his finest clothes so that Emer should see him in his full beauty.

When they reached Forgall's stronghold they saw the girl sitting on the green with her foster-sisters, teaching them needlework. As the girls sat there sewing and talking together, they heard the clatter of hooves, the creaking of a chariot, the crackling of leather harness and the grinding of iron-tyred wheels, heralding the swift approach of an armed warrior.

'Can you see who is coming?' asked Emer.

Fial, Emer's foster-sister, stood up. 'Yes, I can,' she said. 'I see two horses bounding along, rivalling each other in size, in beauty, in valour and in speed. They are galloping side by side, pricking up their sharp ears. Their manes and tails are thick and curling. A grey horse with broad haunches, savage, swift, ruthless, is on the right side of the chariot pole. He thunders along with his head held high and his chest puffed out. The turf beneath his four hard hooves seems to be on fire. The other horse is as black as jet, with a neat head, broad hooves and slender legs. He, too, is full of vigour as he gallops along, stamping hard upon the ground. I see a chariot of fine wood, with wickerwork sides and wheels of white bronze. The chariot-pole is of white silver, mounted with white bronze. The frame is high, its curved yoke golden, with yellow, closely plaited reins. Its shafts are as hard and as straight as the blade of a warrior's sword.'

'I see a man inside the chariot, a dark, thoughtful man with an expression of love on his face. He has a beautiful, five-folded tunic of crimson cloth, fastened with a brooch of inlaid gold. His shirt is white, hooded, with a border of red woven with gold. You would think that a shower of pearls had fallen into his mouth so white and shapely are his teeth. His eye-brows are black as a charred beam. He has a sword with a golden hilt across his thighs, a blood-red spear with a shaft of wood and a bright blade, and a crimson shield with a silver rim chased with patterns of animals in gold. In front of him stands his charioteer, a slender, tall, red-headed man wearing a fillet of bronze on his brow to control his curling hair. He is wearing a short tunic with sleeves slit at the elbows and his goad is made of red gold.'

By now Cu Chulainn had reached the girls and he uttered a blessing on them. Emer lifted up her lovely face and said, 'May the gods smooth your way before you.'
'And you', he replied, 'may you be protected from all harm.'

The two then talked together in strange, unintelligible speech for both knew the secret language of the poets and they did not wish their conversation to be overheard. He described the route he had followed in order to reach her and she in turn told him of the mighty champions who guarded her on every side to prevent her from being carried away from her father's stronghold.
'Don't you think I am a match for them?' he asked.
'I need proof of your valour before I can count you their equal,' she replied.
'I swear on my honour girl,' he said, 'that whenever there is talk of the glories and the strength of heroes, my deeds shall be recounted among them.' Then Cu Chulainn told her about his exploits, about his boyhood among the heroes and druids of Ulster and about his father, Lugh Long Arm of the Tuatha De. 'And as for you, girl, how were you reared?'
'I was brought up in all the ancient virtues,' she answered, 'in lawful behaviour, chastity, with beauty and the rank of a queen, and I have every grace desired in the women of Ireland.'

This pleased Cu Chulainn and he asked Emer why they should not be joined in wedlock. Talking in riddles, she explained that no man might possess her unless he proved his worth by impossible feats of daring but Cu Chulainn was undeterred and accepted all the daunting conditions she made.
'In that case I can accept your offer,' she said.

Then they parted. The other girls told their fathers about the noble youth in the splendid chariot who had talked in such strange speech with Emer and they in turn told Forgall.
'Ah,' he said, 'it is the wild one from Emain Macha who has come looking for Emer and she has fallen in love with him; but I shall come between them.' Forgall had magic powers and he went to Emain in disguise and arranged for Cu Chulainn to be sent away to Scotland to perfect the arts of war under the tuition of the wild war gods and goddesses who lived there. He was certain that Cu Chulainn would never return alive.

So Cu Chulainn crossed to Scotland to learn the arts of war. Although he had many dangerous adventures and escapes from death, his experiences only increased his strength and skills and when the time came for him to return to Ireland and claim Emer, no-one in the world could match him. Forgall had shut himself and

Macha's curse

The great Cattle Raid of Cooley, where Cu Chulainn performed his greatest exploits, involved a struggle between two old enemies, the kingdoms of Connacht and Ulster. Some said that the rivalry began long before, when the Fir Bolg divided Ireland among their tribes; others that it was the Tuatha De who drove the Fir Bolg into Connacht. Whatever the circumstances, by Cu Chulainn's time, Connacht and Ulster were fierce rivals.

Cattle raids and border skirmishes were common and each side had its own champion warriors who were eager to prove their skills. Sometimes the Ulstermen were the victors, sometimes the men of Connacht. At the time of the Cooley raid, however, two important events seemed to favour the Connacht kingdom. The first was the defection of Fergus mac Roich from Ulster to Connacht with a host of followers. Fergus was one of the great warriors of Ulster but he considered that King Conchobar had behaved dishonourably towards him and he now lived in exile and was eager to fight against his old companions. The second, stranger event was a mysterious debility which came over the men of Ulster whenever their kingdom was seriously threatened. This story explains how it came about. The heroine is a woman named Macha, no ordinary woman but a goddess, the equivalent to the Gaulish horse goddess Epona (great mare) and the Welsh Riannon (great queen).

A handsome and wealthy nobleman named Crunnchu mac Agnoman once lived with his four sons in the lonely hills of Ulster. He had been a widower for a long time when one day a beautiful and elegant woman entered the house. Silently, she began to undertake all the domestic chores. She poked the fire and sat by it, but never a word was said. Then she brought the baking board and sieve and began to bake and cook. In the evening, she gave the servants their orders and then sat beside Crunnchu when they ate. Finally, everyone went to bed and when she had put out the fires, she climbed in beside him. She laid her hand upon his side, and so became his wife. After that, Macha and Crunnchu lived

his household inside his strong walled fortress and Cu Chulainn prepared to attack it with his scythed-chariot and all his battle equipage. When he reached the stronghold he leaped its three ramparts like a salmon leaping up three waterfalls and no-one could prevent him. Once inside the fort, he killed twenty-four of the twenty-seven warriors who came to oppose him. The three who escaped were Emer's own brothers. Forgall fled before the furious hero and tried to leap over the ramparts himself but he fell and was mortally wounded. Then Cu Chulainn seized Emer and her foster-sister Fial and, carrying them and their weight in two bags of gold and silver, he leaped once more over the ramparts and made off.

A great cry went up from the onlookers and the pursuit began but Cu Chulainn killed each and every one of his opponents on his journey back to Conchobar's palace. By emerging victorious from all these violent encounters, Cu Chulainn fulfilled all that he had promised to Emer and at nightfall they reached Emain Macha in safety.

Emer was brought to King Conchobar in the House of the Red Branch and presented to the men of Ulster and they welcomed her. Cu Chulainn then made her his wife and they were never again parted while they lived.

together and because of her efforts, Crunnchu became even more prosperous. She delighted in his beauty and soon conceived his child.

On certain important days of the year, the people of Ulster held great gatherings and assemblies which thousands attended, and soon the time came for one of these.

'I will go like everyone else,' Crunnchu said.

'Don't go Crunnchu,' Macha urged, 'you will talk about us and that will bring danger. We can only stay together if you say nothing about me at the gathering.'

'I won't say a word,' he assured her.

The festival was splendid, crowded with people in fine clothes and with fine, spirited horses. There were races and contests, games and processions, and booths of all kinds. The king was there with his druids and the poets chanted his praises. As he passed by, the people shouted, 'The king's horses are the swiftest in the world. There have never been any to match them.'

'My wife runs more quickly than they do,' Crunnchu boasted impetuously, for he had seen his wife running as quickly as the winds across the plains.

'Grab hold of that boaster.' King Conchobar shouted. 'If his wife runs so well, bring her to the race course.'

Crunnchu was tied up and messengers were sent to Macha. She welcomed them graciously and asked them what they wanted.

'We've come to get you so you can free your husband,' they replied, 'he is a prisoner under the king's orders because he boasted that you could out-run his horses.'

'The fool,' she exclaimed, 'he had no right to say that. But as you see, I cannot come: I am about to give birth.'

'If you don't come, they will kill him,' the messengers replied.

'Then I must go with you,' she said simply.

When they arrived, everyone crowded around, anxious to see her.

'It is not decent to stare at me in this condition,' she cried. ' Why was I brought here?'

'To run against the king's horses,' they yelled.

'But my hour is close.'

'Unsheathe your swords, men,' the king commanded, 'and cut that boastful man in pieces.'

'Help me,' Macha cried to the people. 'You have all had a mother.' The crowds ignored her and she turned to the king. 'I beg you Conchobar, grant me respite until after I am delivered.'

'I shall not,' retorted the king.

'Then curse you who have so little pity on me,' she said. 'Because of that you will suffer greater shame than I do now.'

'What is your name?' the king asked curiously.

'My name,' she answered proudly, 'will be the name of this place for ever. I am Macha and I am the daughter of Sainreth mac Imbaith.

Bring the horses level with me!'

The swift horses were brought and the race was run. Macha outstripped the animals easily and with a cry of agony gave birth to twins before any of the horses could reach the winning post. The people who had heard her scream tried to move but suddenly they found they were as weak as a woman in childbed. Then Macha cursed them with her dying breath and said, 'From now on, the shame and disgrace which you have inflicted on me here will be the cause of shame to you all. For when Ulster is in danger, you will become as weak as a woman in labour and as helpless; and this curse will last for nine generations.'

And so it was. The only people not affected by this weakness were the women and children of Ulster and Cu Chulainn, who came from another place. From that time to this, the place where the race was run and where the royal stronghold of Conchobar once stood was known as Emain Macha, or Macha's Twins.

The divine swine-herds

This is the story of two swine-herds who were, in another form, to be the cause of the great cattle raid of Cooley. The pig was the most favoured animal at the Celtic feast and it is not surprising that the swine-herd, like the smith, was held in high regard in Celtic society.

Two of the gods of the Otherworld were Ochall, who ruled the *sidh* of Connacht, and Bodb, who ruled the *sidh* of Munster. Ochall's swine-herd was named Rucht (Grunt) and Bodb's was named Friuch (Bristle) and each looked after a large herd of pigs. These two swine-herds were also druids, and they knew how to practise every druidic art, especially that of transformation. They were great friends and would often graze their pigs together in each other's woods, but eventually a dispute broke out between the people of Connacht and Munster as to which one was the better pig-keeper.

That autumn there was a great harvest of acorns and forest fruits in Munster, and Rucht

brought his pigs south to his friend's woods. After a friendly greeting, Friuch mentioned the dispute.

'They are trying to make trouble between us by saying that your magical power is better than mine,' he said.

'We're about equal,' said Rucht.

'Let's test it,' replied Friuch. 'I shall put a druidic spell on your pigs so that no matter how much they eat, they won't grow fat. Mine will.'

And that's what happened. Rucht's pigs became so thin and emaciated that he was the laughing-stock of everyone.

'I'll invite him to my woods next year,' he swore, 'and I'll trick him in the same way.'

The following autumn Rucht won the contest and now that both herds of pigs were scrawny and starved, everybody admitted that the swine-herds were equal in power. But of course Bodb and Ochall were annoyed at the poor condition of their pigs and the swine-herds were both dismissed.

That finally ended their friendship. They changed themselves into hawks and for two years they fought each other in the skies over the courts of Bodb and Ochall. The noise was tremendous and the people could get no peace. Then they turned into water creatures and fought each other for a year in the river Shannon and another year in the river Suir, but so equal were they that still neither could defeat the other. After that they turned themselves into stags and poached on each other's hinds. Then they fought as warriors, dragons, spirits and finally as eels.

It was while they were in this last shape that they were finally separated. A cow swallowed one of them while she was drinking in a river in Cuailnge (the old name for Cooley) in Ulster; and the other slipped into a well in Connacht and was swallowed by a cow belonging to Queen Medb. After a time the cows each produced a bull calf and these grew into the two great magic bulls, the Donn (the Lordly One) of Cuailnge in Ulster and the white-horned one, the Findbennach in Connacht. To find out what trouble they caused next, you must read the rest of the chapter.

The adventures of Nera

This story begins in Cruachan in Connacht, where Queen Medb and her consort Ailill held court. Most of it is concerned with a mysterious encounter with the Otherworld but at the end the two great bulls appear again, with a hint of trouble to come.

It was Samain, the most dangerous and portentous date in the Celtic year, and a great feast was being prepared in the household of Ailill and Medb in Cruachan, in Connacht. Two captives had been hanged outside the fortress on the previous day and there they still hung, swaying and creaking in the wild wind and darkness. One way to lay their ghosts was to take some twigs from the sacred willow tree and tie a band of twisted twigs around their feet.

Ailill said, 'Anyone who dares to go into the night and tie the willow band around the foot of one of the hanged captives will get whatever he wishes as his prize.'

At Samain the Otherworld was accessible to mortals (at their peril) and the gods played tricks on humans so it needed a lot of courage to fulfil Ailill's dare. One man after another went out to try, but the wind, rain and darkness and also the spectres and demons frightened them all and they hurried back inside the royal stronghold without having even come near the corpses.

'I'll get that prize from you, Ailill,' boasted one of his men named Nera.

'If you do,' said Ailill, 'you shall have my gold-hilted sword as your reward.'

Nera armed himself and went out to the hanged men. Three times he tried to tie the twigs around the foot of one of them, and three times it sprang off. Then the dead man groaned and told him that the band would never stay put unless he fixed it with a proper peg. When this had been done, the dead captive spoke again and said, 'Take me on your back so that I can get a drink for I was very thirsty when they hanged me.'

'Come on then,' replied Nera calmly. 'Where do you want to go?'

'To the nearest house,' replied the corpse. Nera set off carrying the corpse on his back but when they came to the house there was a sea of fire all around it.

'We won't get a drink here,' the dead man said. 'That family has put its fire out. Let us go on.'

They came to another house and there was a lake of water around it.

'That's no good,' said the corpse. 'That family has put all its water pots out. Let us go on.'

They came to a third house, which had no barrier around it and entered. The dead man drank his fill and spat out the rest into the faces of the frightened inhabitants who all fell dead. Then Nera carried the now silent captive back to the gallows and made for Cruachan fortress to claim his reward.

When he arrived there, he found to his horror that while he was away, it had been burned to the ground and that all its people had been beheaded by warriors from the Otherworld. Nera knew that the entrance to the Otherworld was Cruachan Cave and he hurried to it. There he met a troop of Otherworld warriors carrying the heads to their king. Nera was taken to the king. As a captive he was ordered to bring the king a bundle of firewood each day and sent to stay in the house of a single woman.

Nera and the Otherworld woman fell in love and married secretly and he told her the horrors he had seen at the fortress of Cruachan.

'What you saw was an illusion of the gods,' she told him, 'but it will be true unless you warn your people.'

'How can I do that?' Nera asked anxiously.

'Go now, straight to them. They are still sitting around the cauldron feasting, and the fire has not yet been extinguished.'

Yet to Nera, three days and nights had passed since he had entered the Otherworld.

'Tell them that Ailill and Medb must destroy the *sidh* mound at Cruachan cave before two Samains have passed and that they must carry off the precious crown of the king.'

'How can I make them believe I have been in the Otherworld?' Nera asked.

'Take with you the fruits of summer,' she said, for it was the beginning of winter in the human world. 'I shall bear you a son between now and next Samain. Warn me before the raid so that I may save your cattle, your son and your possessions.'

Nera took some wild garlic, primrose and golden fern with him back to the world of mortals and found all was as the woman had foretold. The gold-hilted sword was given to him, and he remained with Ailill and Medb for a year until the time came to return to his wife. She showed him their child and explained that she had carried the firewood for him during the year so that his absence would not be noticed. 'I have given one of the cows to your son,' she said. 'Watch the cattle today.'

Nera guarded the cattle while they grazed but eventually he fell asleep and while he slept, his son's cow was stolen. When he awoke, he managed to overtake the thief, but not before the cow had been mated with a bull—the great bull of Ulster, the Donn of Cuailgne.

After this, Nera returned for another year to the human world. When the feast of Samain came round again, Ailill told Nera to return to the Otherworld and save all his belongings from the *sidh*, for it was about to be destroyed. Nera did as he was advised and stealthily led his cattle out of the cave into the light. The cow that had been stolen the previous year had

produced a strong bull calf and all went well until he left the cave: as he was led out into the air, he bellowed three times with the full force of his lungs.

The great bull of Connacht, the white-horned Findbennach, heard his call and pounded towards them to defend his territory against the upstart. All day the animals fought but they were unevenly matched and at last the calf was beaten. As it lay defeated, it bellowed defiantly. 'What did it say?' Medb asked her druids, for they could understand the language of animals. 'It said that if its father, the Lordly One, the Donn of Cuailnge in Ulster had come to its aid, the white-horned Findbennach would have been beaten all across the plain of Cruachan,' they replied.
'I vow by the gods of my people that I shall not lie down nor sleep on a bed of flock nor drink ale until I see those bulls fighting,' said Medb.

Then the men of Connacht and Fergus and the exiled Ulstermen went to Cruachan Cave and destroyed and plundered it, bringing out the royal crown which is one of the treasures of Ireland. Nera, however, remained behind with his family and he will never return to the world of mortals until the day of doom.

Royal pillow-talk

One night Medb, queen of Connacht, and her consort, Ailill, lay in their bed in their fortress at Cruachan. Ailill said, 'It's a true saying, my love, that the wife of a wealthy man is indeed lucky.'
'That's true, my love, but what made you think of it just now?' replied the queen sleepily.
'I was just thinking how much better off you are now than when you were single,' said Ailill.
'I was very well off before I married you,' Medb retorted. 'My father, the high king of Ireland, gave me the whole province of Connacht to rule. Every man in Ireland wanted me, but I would take only a man free from meanness, cowardice and jealousy.' Then after a while she said, 'I got what I wanted when I married you but I brought you a great dowry and in fact you are a kept man.'

Ailill was annoyed. 'I have two kings for brothers, and would have been a king myself but for my youth. And I've never heard of a province being run by a woman except here.' And so the quarrel grew.

The next morning, they had all their possessions brought to them, and they were found to be equal in all things—except one. Ailill owned the fine white-horned bull, the Findbennach and Medb had no bull to match him. What made it worse for her was that the bull had originally been born to one of her own cows but, scorning to be in a woman's herd, had gone over to Ailill. When she knew she could not rival her husband in this Medb became utterly dejected and all her many possessions were worthless in her eyes. She had to have a bull to equal the Findbennach. She sent for her messenger, Mac Roth, to ask if there was a match for Ailill's bull anywhere in Ireland.
'I know where to get a bull as good or even better,' said Mac Roth. 'He is in Cuailnge in the province of Ulster. He belongs to Daire mac Fiachna and is called the Donn of Cuailnge.'

Medb remembered at once the battle that had taken place between the white-horned Findbennach and the Donn's calf and how the calf had spoken of its father.

'Go there at once and ask his owner to lend him to me for a year so that he can breed on my cows. I'll reward him handsomely.'

Mac Roth led a party to Ulster to negotiate for the bull and his owner, Daire, readily agreed to lend the Donn to Medb for a year. That evening, meat and ale were served in plenty so that Mac Roth and his companions, intoxicated by their success and far too much ale, became drunk and noisy. They began to talk boastfully and one said, 'We'd have taken the bull anyway, even if Daire had refused us.' A servant overheard this and rushed to tell his master.
'I swear by the gods of my people that no part of my property shall leave my land unless I allow it myself,' said Daire. He let matters rest for the night but next morning he flatly refused to give the men of Connacht the bull.
'What is all this about?' asked Mac Roth who had forgotten the boasts of the night before.
'I'll tell you what it's about,' shouted Daire, 'you said that if I had not given my bull willingly you would have taken it by force.'
'What is said at a feast is surely beneath your notice,' said Mac Roth.
'Nor is it the fault of Medb and Ailill.'

'Where have you come from?' Medb asked. 'From Scotland, where I have been learning the arts of poetry and druidism.'
'Have you the power to see into the future?' Medb asked.
'I have,' replied the girl.
'Then druidess,' Medb said eagerly, 'tell me, what will become of my army?'

The girl gazed ahead of her and then replied, 'I see crimson, I see red.'
'No that cannot be so,' cried Medb. 'I have heard that the men of Ulster are powerless under the curse of weakness and cannot resist me. Now tell me Fedelm, how do you see my army?'
'I see crimson, I see red,' repeated the druidess.
'Wrong,' shouted the queen, 'many of Ulster's warriors are on service elsewhere and Fergus mac Roich is here in exile with us with his three thousand men. Druidess, how do you see our army?'
'I see crimson, I see red,' Fedelm persisted.
'Well, that doesn't mean anything,' said Medb. 'There are bound to be wounds and blood in a battle. So, for the last time, prophetess, tell me what you see.'
'I see crimson, I see red.' Then the girl chanted a prophetic lyric which foretold the victory of the Hound, Cu Chulainn, and the utter defeat of the armies of Connacht.

Medb, however, was determined and, although she could not forget that gloomy prophecy she gave the order to advance towards Ulster where Cu Chulainn lay in wait for them.

Cu Chulainn and Ferdiad

Confident that the men of Ulster lay helpless under Macha's curse, Medb led her army deep into Ulster. She did not know, however, that Cu Chulainn was unaffected, and that, young as he was, he was determined to defend the province until the warriors recovered.

As the men of Connacht advanced, Cu Chulainn harried them relentlessly, ambushing them and killing a hundred every day. At last Medb in desperation agreed to halt her army

'Never mind,' said Daire, 'the bull stays here.'

There was nothing the messengers could do but return to Connacht with the bad news. 'Well, we needn't lose sleep over it.' said Medb. 'He knew very well that if he didn't give us the bull willingly we would take him by force. And taken he will be.'

And that is how the great war of the Cattle Raid of Cooley started between the men of Ulster and the Men of Connacht.

Medb and Ailill gathered a great army from the four provinces of Ireland to seize the Donn of Cuailnge, but they could not advance into Ulster until their druids saw that the signs were favourable. After two weeks they pronounced the omens to be good and the army assembled, with Medb in the forefront in her chariot. She was about to give the command to advance when she saw a young girl in front of them. She was yellow-haired and very beautiful and her dress was that of a noblewoman. She was standing in a splendid chariot drawn by two fine, jet-black steeds, and in her hand was a golden, druidic wand.
'Who are you,' cried Medb. 'I am Fedelm, a druidess,' she replied.

and to send a warrior each day to fight in single combat with Cu Chulainn at a nearby ford. It made no difference. Although he was only seventeen years old, Cu Chulainn overcame Medb's greatest champions and none could get the better of him.

Even Fergus mac Roich, the exiled Ulster hero, was forced to meet him. The love between the two was too strong, however, to allow them to harm one another and they agreed to fight a sham battle. It was arranged that Cu Chulainn would pretend to run away, on the understanding that next time they met in battle, Fergus would do the same. In this way Fergus could not be accused of disloyalty to his adopted homeland; but Cu Chulainn still defended the ford.

Medb was increasingly alarmed. She decided that the only man able to match Cu Chulainn was his beloved foster-brother, Ferdiad, who, like Fergus, was in exile with the men of Connacht. At first Ferdiad refused to fight for the boys had been brought up together and the bond between them was stronger even than that between brothers. It was only when Medb convinced Ferdiad that Cu Chulainn had spoken contemptuously of him that he agreed.

So Ferdiad and Cu Chulainn came face to face in the middle of the ford.
'Welcome Cu Chulainn,' Ferdiad said.
'It is for me to welcome you, Ferdiad,' retorted the Hound. 'You are on my home territory remember, and you should not have challenged me to combat.' Then they began to belittle each other and their anger rose until they had forgotten their love and the fights and adventures they had been through together.

At length Ferdiad said, 'We have said enough. What weapons shall we choose today?'
'Since you arrived first,' said the Hound, 'you have the choice of weapons.'

They fought fiercely all day, and by nightfall both were drenched in blood. Exhausted, they flung their arms around each other's necks and kissed each other three times. That night they slept in the same field and Cu Chulainn's physicians placed magic healing herbs in both warriors' wounds. The men of Connacht sent food and soothing drinks to Ferdiad, and he gave to Cu Chulainn half of everything.

For two more days they fought on foot and each day received terrible wounds; but at night they were healed by magic herbs and their strength was revived by the finest food and drink. The next day they fought with their horses and chariots but though by nightfall both horses and men were near to death, neither could claim a victory.

Finally the day came when they knew that one or both must fall. Cu Chulainn arrived at the ford and saw Ferdiad practising his swordsmanship there. Cu Chulainn turned to his charioteer.
'Look Laeg,' he said, 'he is going to use those frightening tricks on me today. If I am losing, you must mock me and anger me to greater effort. If I am winning, then urge me on so that I do not falter.' Then he put on his battle armour and the two men fought more fiercely than on any day before.

When it was time for Cu Chulainn to choose the method of fighting, he said 'Let us fight in the water of the ford,' and Ferdiad's heart sank because he knew that no-one had yet escaped Cu Chulainn in the water.

Never was such a single combat seen by either side and as the day drew on, a great battle madness seized both warriors. Cu Chulainn leaped onto the rim of Ferdiad's shield to strike through his head and Ferdiad sent the shield flying so that Cu Chulainn was flung onto the bank of the ford. He sprang up only to be thrown down once more and Laeg, sensing his master was failing, mocked him to spur him on. Next Ferdiad struck Cu Chulainn a blow that pierced his breast and Cu Chulainn knew that if he was to win, he would have to use a deadly weapon which only he could wield and from which no-one could escape.
'Bring me the pronged spear, Laeg,' he shouted.

Laeg floated the great pronged spear downstream and Cu Chulainn caught it with his foot and sent it hurtling towards Ferdiad. Ferdiad had moved his shield to protect the lower part of his body and the spear ripped into his chest, its fierce barbs penetrating deep into his body.
'You have finished me,' screamed Ferdiad, and

he fell dead into the river. Cu Chulainn ran to him, lifted him in his arms and carried him to the bank. As he laid him gently down, he nearly fainted himself not only from his own wounds, but from his grief at the death of his foster-brother. Sadly he ordered Laeg to retrieve the deadly pronged spear. Then, seeing the weapon stained crimson by Ferdiad's blood, he sang a lament for the lost companion of his boyhood.

Lugh aids his wounded son

That night Cu Chulainn lay near to death and Laeg watched over him. The charioteer was near to despair when he saw a man approaching and asked Cu Chulainn who it could be. 'What is he like?' said Cu Chulainn, who could not raise his head to look for himself.
'That's an easy question,' replied Laeg. 'He is very tall and handsome with yellow, curling hair. He has a green cloak wrapped about him and fastened with a brooch of gleaming silver, and under it a silken tunic which reaches to his knees. He carries a mighty, single-edged sword and two spears, one with five barbs: his shield is black with a hard edge of silvered bronze. But the strange thing is that no-one takes any notice of him, nor does he look at anyone. It is as if no-one else can see him.'
'It is someone from the Otherworld who has taken pity on me for they know that I alone am fighting against the four provinces of Ireland.'
The young warrior came up to Cu Chulainn and spoke to him, telling him how sad he was about his terrible task, his long lack of sleep, and his fearful wounds.
'But,' he said, 'I will help you.'
'Who are you?' asked Cu Chulainn.
'I am your father from the Otherworld, Lugh Long Arm. So sleep Cu Chulainn. I myself will fight your battle.' Then he sang Cu Chulainn into a deep and tranquil sleep and placed healing herbs from the Otherworld into all the cuts and wounds on his son's broken body. While Cu Chulainn slept, the god Lugh fought in his likeness and within a few days, the young warrior was restored and ready to fight again.

The last battle

Cu Chulainn fought single-handed against the men of Ireland from Samain on 1 November until the feast of Imbolc on 1 February. Then at last the Ulstermen began to recover from their sickness and Conchobar mac Nessa led his great armies to relieve his exhausted nephew and to fight against Medb and her army. They met at nightfall and agreed a truce until dawn. Cu Chulainn was suffering again from fresh wounds and he lay helpless in a nearby fort, held down by wooden hoops and ropes to restrain him from the coming battle.
At dawn, the men of Ulster prepared to fight. As was the custom among the Celts, they were all stark naked except for their weapons and shields and their battle cries rang out across the plain.
On the Connacht side, Fergus was finally persuaded to fight for the people among whom he had made his home and, crying out that he would sever men's heads until they lay on the ground thicker than hailstones in a storm, he entered the battle. Conchobar soon noticed that a new force had entered the battle and he confronted Fergus on the field.
'I drove you into exile to live with mad dogs and foxes and I'll stop your treacherous tricks with my own hand this day before all the men of Ireland.' Fergus lunged at him with his sword but Cormac, Conchobar's son, seized his arm. 'Steady, steady,' he said soothingly, 'do not wield your sword against the men of Ulster. Think of your honour.'
'I must strike three mighty blows on the Ulstermen this day,' cried Fergus in a frenzy from the battle.
'Then strike off the tops of the hills over the heads of the warriors,' suggested Cormac. 'That will settle your rage.'
So Fergus turned and with his mighty sword struck off the tops of the three hills which overlooked the plain. They landed with a deafening crash in the marshy lowlands of Meath and there they can still be seen today. 'Who made that noise?' Cu Chulainn asked Laeg, who was beside him. When he learned, he tore off the hoops and ropes that held him,

scattering the coverings from his wounds and
the sphagnum moss with which they were
packed. His war-frenzy came on him and, as his
weapons had been taken away, he seized hold
of his chariot, lifted it onto his back and roared
into the battle, using it as a battering ram to
force his way through the throng to Fergus.
'I swear by the gods of Ulster that if you do not
get away from here, I shall grind you down as a
mill grinds good hard grain,' he shouted.
'Who is the man in Ireland who dares to talk to
me like that?' Fergus cried.
'I am the Hound of Ulster, your foster-son and
Conchobar mac Nessa's foster-son. You

promised you would flee from me when next
you met me in battle,' replied Cu Chulainn,
reminding him of the promise they had made
when they met in single combat.

At once Fergus turned and in three great
strides left the battlefield, taking with him his
troop of three thousand men and all the men of
the other provinces of Ireland so that Ailill and
Medb with the men of Connacht were left alone
to fight the Ulstermen.

By sunset, Cu Chulainn had smashed the last
company of Connachtmen and held Medb
herself at his mercy. But as he had come on
her from behind, he thought it unfair to strike.

'Grant me a favour today, Cu Chulainn,' she begged.

'What is it that you want?' he replied.

'That my army may be under your protection until they have gone westwards over the border.

'I shall grant it' he said.

Now although Cu Chulainn did not know it, Medb had sent her men behind the enemy lines and they had already captured the Lordly One, the Donn of Cuailnge and sent him to Connacht by a different track with fifty heifers and eight cattlemen. Medb might have lost the battle, but she had taken the bull as she had boasted.

'It is the fate of a herd led by a mare that has befallen the men of Connacht today,' said Fergus bitterly, returning to survey the dead and wounded on the battle field. 'Total disaster.'

So ended the famous Cattle Raid of Cooley, where Cu Chulainn, the Hound of Ulster, fought single-handed against the might of Ireland. And what happened to the bulls, the cause of all the fighting and bloodshed? Their story follows next.

The battle of the bulls

When the Donn of Cuailnge came to the beautiful, unfamiliar land of Connacht, he gave three mighty bellows and the great white-horned Findbennach heard them. No other bull in Connacht dared make a sound louder than a cow's gentle moo and, sensing a challenge to his supremacy, the Findbennach tossed his noble head with its great horns wildly in the air and advanced to Cruachan, Medb's fort, to meet his rival.

Every able-bodied person ran to witness that awesome confrontation, even the men of Ulster now that there was peace again. Someone had to judge the battling bulls and Bricriu mac Garbada was chosen, because he was known to be equally fair to friend and foe. He stood nearby at a place where he could see both sides clearly.

As soon as the bulls spotted each other they lowered their heads and began to paw the ground, sending great sods of earth flying like black birds from under their heavy hooves. Their eyes blazed like torches, their nostrils swelled and distended, and they charged at each other with a mighty, wicked rush. They pierced and they gored and they ripped and they mangled one another. The Findbennach soon realized he had the advantage: the Donn was tired from his long journey and was in a strange country. At the next charge, he thrust his white horn viciously into his rival's side. The force of the impact carried the bulls to where Bricriu was watching them and they trampled him to death under their lashing hooves.

Cormac, son of Conchobar, saw what was happening and he struck the Donn three great blows between his ear and his tail.

'You weren't worth fighting over,' he shouted. 'You cannot match a calf half your age.'

The Donn, like the Findbennach, had human understanding and these scathing words incensed him. He made a great attack on the Findbennach and the bulls fought again fiercely for many hours. When darkness fell, only the terrifying thunder of hooves and the snorting of the fighting bulls could be heard. That night they circled the whole of Ireland and at dawn the Donn of Cuailnge returned from the west with the mangled remains of the Findbennach dangling from his horns.

After this, no-one dared to stand in his way and he rampaged through all Ireland, tossing his huge horns and shaking bits of the Findbennach off them at places which still bear their names. Then he turned north again and made for Cuailnge, his own land. When he arrived, he came to a small hill and there his great heart shattered like a nut in his breast and he lay down and died from the great effort of his fighting. Ever since then, the hill has been called *Druim Tairb*, The Ridge of the Bulls.

So perished the Findbennach, 'the white horned bull of Connacht', and the Lordly One, the Donn of Cuailnge, the two great bulls that were the cause of the Cattle Raid of Cooley. And so perished, too, the spirits of the two swine-herds who had fought one another for so long among the hills and plains of Ireland.

The story of Fionn

In the ancient Celtic world there were two classes of warrior. The first were warriors within the tribe, heroes who obeyed the tribal laws and kept to the manners and customs of their people even when, like Cu Chulainn, they were descended from the gods.

The second class of warriors were very different: they were *ecland* or tribeless and lived outside the tribe, obedient only to their own laws but recognized as being an important though separate part of society. The outlaws formed themselves into groups known as *Fian* or Fenians, which means 'war', 'battle'.

The Fenians lived in the twilit borders between the supernatural and the real worlds and for them the two worlds were each as real and tangible as the other. In human form they were recruited from among the aristocracy, choosing to undergo daunting initiation rites and ordeals in order to qualify for membership of the group. Once admitted, however, they were able to travel freely into the Otherworlds, taking on animal forms and characteristics at will. They were of more than human size and their adventures often involved them in tasks beyond the skills of ordinary mortals.

The most famous of all the Fenians was Fionn, the son of Cumhall. Some time before he was born, his father quarrelled with another outlaw over the leadership of the Fenian bands in Ireland. A fierce battle was fought in which Cumhall was killed by a man named Goll mac Morna, who, himself blinded in one eye, carried off Cumhall's head and all his possessions. So began a feud between the family of Cumhall and the family of Morna which was to last for the rest of their lives.

Stories about Fionn and the Fenians have been told for hundreds of years. They were written down in some of the very earliest Irish manuscripts and can still be heard today in parts of Ireland and the Scottish highlands. At one time it was believed that Fionn was based on a historical character but most scholars now think he is a a more supernatural being, a survivor of the old gods of the Gaels.

Fionn was still in his mother's womb when his father Cumhall was killed at the battle of Cnucha. When he was born, his mother named him Demne and, fearing that he would be sought out and killed by his father's enemies, sent him away to be brought up by

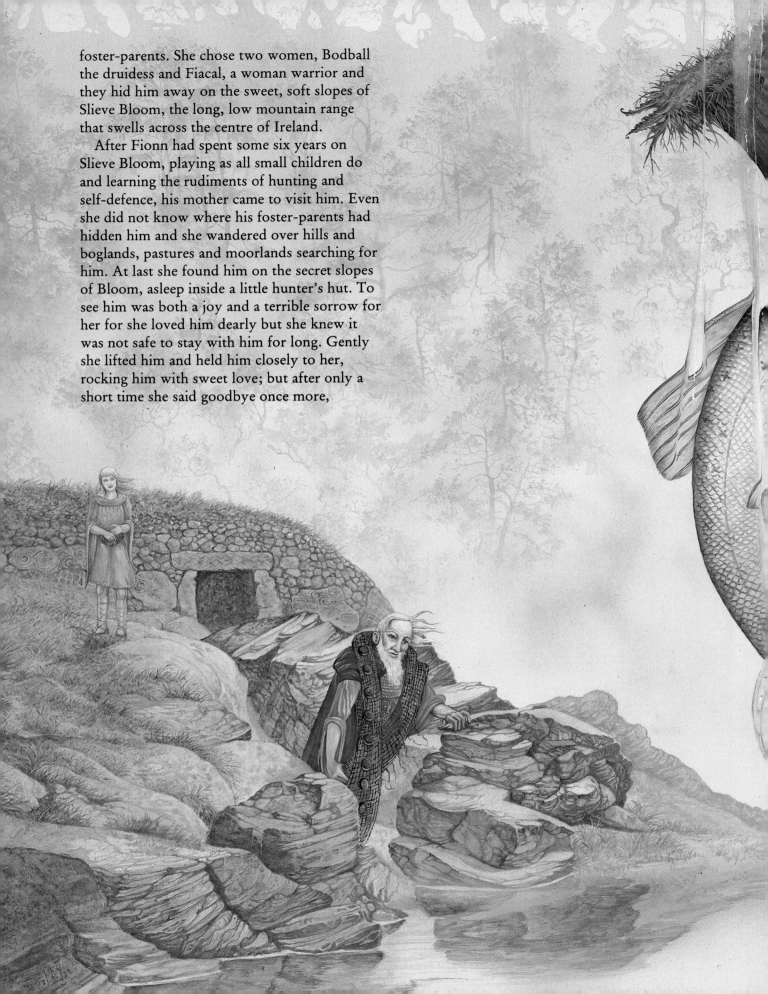

foster-parents. She chose two women, Bodball the druidess and Fiacal, a woman warrior and they hid him away on the sweet, soft slopes of Slieve Bloom, the long, low mountain range that swells across the centre of Ireland.

After Fionn had spent some six years on Slieve Bloom, playing as all small children do and learning the rudiments of hunting and self-defence, his mother came to visit him. Even she did not know where his foster-parents had hidden him and she wandered over hills and boglands, pastures and moorlands searching for him. At last she found him on the secret slopes of Bloom, asleep inside a little hunter's hut. To see him was both a joy and a terrible sorrow for her for she loved him dearly but she knew it was not safe to stay with him for long. Gently she lifted him and held him closely to her, rocking him with sweet love; but after only a short time she said goodbye once more,

instructing the foster-mothers to care for him until he was old enough to take arms and become a warrior. The two women fulfilled their promise well and in these quiet forests, remote from the inhabited lands of Ireland, the boy grew in strength and wisdom, receiving a splendid training in the arts of war and magic.

One day, Demne decided to try his hand at hunting by himself and went off to a lake where he had often seen ducks swimming. His aim was so accurate and his sling-stone so sharp that when it struck one of the ducks it cut off all its wing feathers so that it could not fly away. Proudly the boy carried it home alive to his foster-mothers, evidence of his very first hunting expedition.

As he grew, he became bored with the company of the two women and ran off with a band of wandering poets and scholars. Later he lived with a notorious robber in the south of Ireland. But all this time he told no-one who he was, living in fear of his father's killers, the sons of Morna. Eventually his foster-mothers discovered where he was hiding and took him back north with them to the secret slopes of Slieve Bloom.

Before long, however, he crept out by himself once more. This time he made his way to a place called the Plain of Life where there was a fortress and where he could see the boys of the household playing a game of shinty on the green. He went up to them and challenged them to individual contests in running and shinty, winning each one easily. He returned the next day to find a quarter of their number ranged against him and still he beat them all. Next day a third of them played against him and then, since he was still an easy winner, they made him take on the whole group together. He defeated them utterly.
'What is your name?' they asked him at last.
'Demne,' he answered.

The boys complained about him to the chief of the household. 'We cannot do anything against him,' they said.
'Did he tell you who he is?' asked the chieftain.
'Yes, Demne,' they replied.
'What does he look like?' asked the chieftain.
'He is a strong, fair lad.'

'Well then,' replied the chieftain, 'let him have a name to suit his looks. I shall call him Fionn,' (for *fionn* means 'fair' in old Irish).

Fionn returned again and again to try his skills against the boys of the fortress but he never found his match among them. At home, too, his hunting skills outstripped the skills of his foster-mothers and soon he was doing all the hunting for them. At last the time came when they said he must leave them. His exploits were becoming known and they feared that the sons of Morna would soon discover who and where he was.

At first he entered the service of the King of Bantry but before long, fearing that his skills would give away his identity, he moved to the court of the King of Kerry. This king quickly realized who the tall, fair warrior must be and sent him away. 'You are Cumhall's son,' he said, 'the man the sons of Morna have hunted for many a year. You must not stay here for they will find you out and it would not do if you were slain while under my protection.'

So Fionn made his way through Ireland, fighting with marauding monsters and challenging robbers and warriors to single combat. In those days it was not enough for a warrior to be strong and skilled in war; the true hero must also learn the arts of poetry and Fionn came to study with an old poet whose name was Finneces. The old man lived by the slow-flowing, broad-banked River Boyne and had spent seven years beside a pool where it was said the sacred salmon of knowledge lurked. It had been prophesied that a man named Fionn would catch and eat the salmon and that when he did, he would gain knowledge of all things. Finneces considered his name was so close to the name in the prophecy that he must be the one it meant.

Not long after Fionn arrived, the old poet managed to catch the salmon and he ordered his pupil to cook it, making sure he did not eat a scrap of it himself.
'Have you eaten any of it?' he asked suspiciously when Fionn brought the cooked fish.
'No,' replied Fionn, 'but I burned my thumb on it and I sucked it to stop the pain.'

'What is your name, boy?' asked the old poet.
'Demne.'
'Is that your only name?'
'They call me Fionn.'
'Then eat the salmon, Fionn. It is yours by right.'

So Fionn ate the salmon of knowledge and became the all knowing one. From that time on, whenever he put his thumb in his mouth, he could see into the future and knew the fate of the world.

Armed not only with strength but with wisdom and with the counsel of the gods, Fionn at last defeated his enemies, the sons of Morna and took his place as king of the Fenians.

Diarmuid and Grainne

There are many stories about the exploits of Fionn and the Fenians and of how they rid the land of Ireland of its monsters and plagues. Usually Fionn is portrayed as the wisest, most generous of men but in this famous tale he is shown in a strangely grim and harsh light. It is a story in which both gods and mortals are involved for Diarmuid, one of its principal characters, was the foster-son of Angus, the Irish god of love. It is one of the most popular tales still to be heard in Gaelic Scotland and the lament of Grainne on Diarmuid's death is still sung with deep feeling in the Highlands and Islands of the north.

The story begins when Fionn is already an old man with grown children of his own.

Fionn now wished to marry again and the girl he chose was Grainne, whose father was Cormac, King of Ireland. The king happily agreed to the match although his daughter was young and beautiful whereas Fionn was an old man. Fionn and his men duly arrived at the king's court of Tara. There were many fine warriors in Fionn's entourage but the best and most handsome was Diarmuid, grandson of Duibhne, from whom the Campbells of Scotland claim descent. Diarmuid had an extra advantage when dealing with women: on his brow he had a dark love spot and any woman who saw it fell hopelessly in love with him. To avoid this embarrassment, Diarmuid always wore his helmet pulled well down over his forehead when in the company of women.

On the day the Fenians arrived at Tara, Diarmuid was left on guard while the other men went off to hunt. The day was hot and beads of perspiration were soon streaming down his face. Thinking that he was alone, he raised his helmet to wipe his brow. Grainne, who was already half in love with him, was watching him secretly and from the moment she saw the love spot on his forehead, she thought only of him.

When the warriors returned to Tara, Grainne was taken to meet Fionn.
'Why have I been brought here?' she asked a druid.
'Fionn wishes to marry you,' he told her.
'It surprises me,' she answered, 'that he doesn't

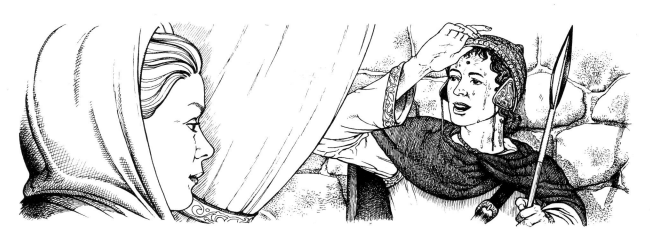

give me to his son Oisin. He is nearer my age:
Fionn is older than my father.'

'It is Fionn who wants you for his wife,' the
druid said.

Grainne, however, was determined to marry
whom she pleased. She mixed a potion that
would have knocked out nine men and at the
feast that evening she added it to some mead
and presented it to Fionn and his chief warriors,
carefully avoiding giving any to Diarmuid.
They all drank it and immediately collapsed
into a deep, drunken sleep. Grainne crept up to
Diarmuid.

'Come away with me,' she said urgently.

'That I will not,' he answered. 'I cannot touch a
woman who is betrothed to Fionn.'

'All right,' she said. 'I shall put you under a
druidic spell of such power that you will be
forced to do as I say and that quickly, before
Fionn wakes from his drunken sleep.'

'You are a wicked woman,' said Diarmuid, 'but
I cannot come with you for Fionn has the keys
of the fortress tonight so we cannot get out.'

'There's a wicker gate that will be open,' she
insisted.

'It is tabu for me to pass through a wicker gate.'

'Then use your spear to vault over the ramparts
and I will meet you outside.'

Diarmuid was already under her power and
when she added 'I won't give you up until I
die,' he agreed to her plan.

'Then I'll come with you without the need for
spells,' he told her.

Together they fled from the castle and so
began their exile.

It was not long before Fionn discovered what
had happened and set out in a jealous fury to
capture them. At first the runaways hid in a
wood, living in a hut of branches, protected by
a strong fence with seven doors. When Fionn
and his men surrounded them, Diarmuid's
foster-father, the god Angus, offered to wrap
them both in his cloak of invisibility so that
they could escape but Diarmuid at first chose to
stand and fight. Grainne, however, was led
away unseen into the forest.

Fionn ordered his men to guard the seven
doors to Diarmuid's fence, standing at the
seventh himself. Only when he knew he would

have to fight against his leader did Diarmuid
make his escape. With a mighty leap he cleared
the fence and ran like the wind to the place
where Grainne was hidden.

Helped by Angus, the couple managed to live
hidden in the countryside, moving continually
from place to place and suffering terrible
hardships. Still Fionn pursued them and at last,
when Grainne became pregnant, they took
refuge near a sacred rowan tree that was
guarded by a savage giant. The giant was so
fierce that usually not even the Fenians dared to
approach him but Diarmuid was desperate. To
his surprise, the giant allowed the pair to live
nearby as long as they did not attempt to eat
any berries from the tree.

All went well until Grainne developed an unbearable craving for the berries of the sacred tree. She tried to hide her longing but eventually Diarmuid found out. He asked the giant to allow Grainne to eat some of the fruit, but he refused angrily. Worried that Grainne would grow ill with longing, Diarmuid fought the giant and after a fierce battle, managed to kill him. Grainne ate her fill of the berries and for a time they lived peacefully again, taking over the giant's home in the branches of the tree.

It was not long before Fionn heard of the giant's death and, guessing that it was the work of Diarmuid, he camped with his men at the foot of the tree.

Fionn sat down in the shade of the tree and said, 'Fetch the chess board so that Oisin and I may have a game.'

Fionn was the best chessplayer in the world, because whenever he was in trouble he put his thumb in his mouth and knew which the best move was. Diarmuid watched the game from his home in the tree and soon saw that Oisin was in trouble. He could not bear to see his friend lose so he dropped a rowan berry onto the piece Oisin needed to move. Oisin moved it and began to win the game. Eventually Fionn regained his advantage so Diarmuid dropped another rowan berry onto the board.

Fionn was suspicious. 'This looks like Diarmuid's doing,' he said and, looking up into the branches, saw Diarmuid and Grainne hidden among the leaves.

The two were trapped but once more Angus came to help them.

'Take Grainne under your cloak of invisibility and carry her away,' Diarmuid urged. 'I will come to you when I can.'

Angus at once spirited Grainne away and Diarmuid ran along a branch until he was beyond the circle of Fionn's warriors, jumped to the ground and managed to outrun them. The lovers were safe again.

Grainne gave birth to a girl child and as the years passed, she decided it was time for a reconciliation with Fionn. Many of Fionn's warriors privately sympathized with the lovers and Fionn was persuaded to receive them back.

However, although Fionn apparently forgave them, he was only pretending and was in fact determined to have his revenge.

In those days a poisonous boar lurked in the rocky places near where Fionn and his men were living. All the young, brave hunters who had tried to kill it had failed and many had met their own deaths in the attempt. With treachery in his heart, Fionn asked Diarmuid to hunt it down and, to Fionn's amazement and anger, Diarmuid managed to kill the savage monster.

When they brought the skin of the great boar to him, Fionn said, 'You have done well; but what does it measure?'

'I'll see,' said Diarmuid and this was the trap. He paced out the length of the skin with his bare feet and as he did so, the poisonous bristles pierced his foot and he fell into a faint. When he recovered consciousness, Fionn was standing over him.

'Heal me, Fionn,' he begged. 'When you ate the salmon of wisdom you were given the gift of healing. Let me drink from your palms and be cured.'

'You don't deserve that,' Fionn retorted but then he remembered Diarmuid's years of loyal service and changed his mind.

Three times Fionn went to fetch water from a nearby well. Each time, when he thought of his faithful warrior, Diarmuid, he hurried towards him, holding the water carefully in his cupped hands; but each time he thought of Grainne he let the water slip between his fingers. By the time he had finally decided to give Diarmuid the healing drink, it was too late. Diarmuid was dead.

Fionn's companions were furious with him for tricking Diarmuid after peace had been made between them. The only way he could keep his authority as their leader was by comforting the grief-stricken Grainne. At first she would not listen and tore his heart with her bitter words but Fionn persisted and eventually won her over.

Fionn and Grainne became man and wife and remained so until the end of their days. But although Grainne forgot her hatred of the man who had brought her so much sorrow, she never forgot her love for Diarmuid.

The death of Fionn

Fionn had led the Fenians of Ireland for many years and had himself eventually slain his father's killer, Goll mac Morna. There was no-one to rival him in feats of daring, in magic and poetry and in wisdom and he was respected and obeyed everywhere. However, many years earlier a prophecy had been made that Fionn would die in Ireland in a certain year and when that year arrived, Fionn prudently decided to leave for Scotland.

His men protested when they heard the news and said, 'Fionn, have we not meat and drink enough to feast you in Ireland for a whole year? We will take it in turns to feed and entertain you each night in our own dwellings in a manner fit for the Fenian king.' Fionn was touched by their affection and could not bring himself to refuse their offer.

By chance, the first household to provide him with hospitality was that of Fer-tai whose wife was Goll mac Morna's daughter. Their son, Fer-li, took after his grandfather Goll in physical strength and daring, and had never forgiven Fionn for his grandfather's death. When Fionn came to Fer-tai's household, he had only a small band of warriors with him, and seeing this Fer-li gathered together a group of his own kinsmen to hatch a plot.

Fionn billeted most of his men outside the fort and found when he entered it that a splendid feast was ready for him. The hall was hung with fine fabrics, the floor was strewn with sweet-smelling rushes and there was a great fire burning in the centre of the room.

He was sitting at the long feasting table with his chief warriors when he heard a great uproar and saw a group of men approaching belligerently. They accused Fionn's men of killing the local cattle and even the farmers themselves.

'We do not care for these raids,' shouted Fer-li. 'Don't worry,' said Fionn soothingly. 'I will give you two cows for each one stolen, and the same for any sheep and horses.' He knew the report was a lie, to excuse an attack on him and his men.

'You did not come here in peace,' shouted

Fer-li. 'You have come to slay us just as you slew our fathers and our grandfathers before us.' And he attacked Fionn in a frenzy of rage. Then Fionn and his warriors rose as one man and fierce fighting broke out in the hall.

Fer-tai tried to get matters under control and to protect Fionn, his invited guest, but no-one listened to him and twenty-seven fine warriors had fallen before his wife heard the commotion and came rushing into the hall with her patterned scarf torn from her head and her breasts bared as a sign of peace. She upbraided her son severely.

'My son,' she cried, 'it is a betrayal of soldierly honour and an omen of ill-fortune for you to try to betray the illustrious Fionn here in our own stronghold. Get out at once.'

As he obeyed his mother's command, Fer-li shouted at Fionn, 'I challenge you to battle at

the battlefield. This is nothing but folly.'

'It is battle or nothing,' raged Fer-li, sending Birgad back with a sneer. 'Tell that to the feeble, worn-out old man.'

'By my word,' Fionn snarled when he heard the message, 'I swear I will do battle with them like a stripling.' However, he sent Birgad back with a last attempt at peace which Fer-li refused haughtily.

Then the King of the Fenians of Ireland rose and slowly put on his battle dress. Over a thin shirt of finest silk he donned his waxed, cotton shirts, his coat of iron chain-mail and his decorated, gold-bordered breastplate. He put on a stout corselet which reached from his thighs to his armpits. His five-edged spears were placed on one side and his gold-hilted sword lay ready on the other. His shield, decorated with marvellous designs and colours, was strapped on his back. On his head he placed a golden helmet inset with glowing gems.

So he stood dressed for battle, like a great tree under which his warriors could take shelter and so he strode with firm, angry steps towards the ford. No-one who saw him could wonder why it was that he should be king of all the Fenians. He had fought for the good of Ireland all his life; he had saved his beloved land from many invasions and even from a great plague and he was by now more than 230 years old.

Undaunted by the great army ranged against him the old man led his men to battle, inciting them on to brave and heroic deeds. At the familiar, well-loved voice of their king the hundred and fifty Fenians prepared for battle in high spirits. Raising a forest of flaming spears, they formed together into a close-knit band, protected by their glittering, many coloured shields.

Trumpets were blown, wild war-cries rang out through the countryside, and without pausing for an instant the two armies hurled themselves against each other. The echoes of their frenzied shouts rang out in the lush woods and craggy slopes, penetrating the deepest caves and the most tranquil estuaries. Then sharp-edged thrusting spears were used and deadly casting spears and heavy sling stones were hurled towards the enemy lines.

Ath Bres tomorrow, Fionn.'

Fer-li's challenge was accepted and early next morning, Fionn and his 150 men went to the ford at Ath Bres on the River Boyne. There they could see Fer-tai and Fer-li leading 3000 men in battle formation. Dismayed at the unequal numbers, Fionn sent a woman, Birgad, to offer generous peace terms.

Fer-tai would have accepted them gladly, but his son was determined that there would be a battle.

'Accept the terms,' advised Fer-tai, 'for Fionn loves you dearly. You were never away from his household when you were young.'

'Fionn and I shall never take a drink together again,' Fer-li said angrily, 'nor shall I ever enter his house again.'

'That is foolish,' said Fer-tai. 'Fionn is a noble, splendid prince, full of strength and courage on

The fierce fighting went on until at last the brave band of Fenians was defeated, outnumbered by the hordes of Fer-li's men. In the middle of the battle, Fionn himself was seen to fall dead and the descendants of the clan of Morna waved their spears in victory and sang their songs of triumph.

Fionn and many of his fine warriors seemed to perish but we know that this was not in fact so. The Otherworld people came secretly to aid them, carrying the Fenians off to their *sidh* mounds for healing and rest. There they lie to this day, fast asleep with their horses and their weapons beside them, waiting until they are awakened by the sound of trumpets proclaiming that their beloved country is in danger. Then they will rise again in the full strength of their valour and will seize their weapons, rouse their horses and emerge from underground caverns to defend their people as they did in days gone by.

The old men

Long after Fionn had disappeared from the land of Ireland, Saint Patrick travelled through the country on his great mission, bringing Christianity to the pagan Celts. On his journey it is said that he met two ancient men, the only survivors of the great Fenian bands: Oisin, the son of Fionn and Caoilte mac Ronan, one of Fionn's closest friends and best warriors. It happened like this.

One night, as the clouds of evening veiled the soft sides and wooded slopes of sweet Slieve Bloom, everyone was downcast and depressed. Caoilte said to Oisin, 'Now, old friend, where do you suggest we go for entertainment?'
'I cannot say,' replied Oisin sadly, 'there are so few of us good companions left alive now.'

They spent that night and the next two at the house of Cama, who had looked after Oisin when he was a boy. During the day they pretended to be cheerful in front of her as she, too, was unhappy, but at night they wept openly and talked nostalgically of the good days now long since past. On the third day they wandered out of the enclosure and resolved that the only thing to do was to part.

Oisin and his men went to the *sidh* mound where his mother lived. Caoilte and his men went southwards over Magh Breg to the fort of Drum Derg where Saint Patrick was chanting the Mass and blessing the stronghold which had once belonged to Fionn mac Cumhall.

When the holy men saw the band of huge, old men approaching them and noted the great size of their hunting dogs, they were quite terrified; these were clearly beings from another age. Then Patrick bravely seized the holy water carrier and sprinkled them all with holy water. What a hoard of sprites and demons flew out of them then!
'That's better,' said Patrick. 'Who are you?'
'I am Caoilte, son of Ronan,' Caoilte replied. The holy men ventured closer, still amazed by the size of the men. Even when the Fenians were sitting down, the tallest of the holy men only came up to their waists. Then Patrick said, 'I'm going to ask you a favour Caoilte,' and Caoilte replied, 'I don't know if I have the

strength left for it, but what is it, Patrick?'
'I want to find a well of pure water near here so that I can baptize the tribes of Breg, of Meath and of Usnech.'
'I'll bring you to it,' answered Caoilte readily. He led the priests over the bank of the stronghold, and taking Patrick's cross in his hand, pointed out a spring with a clear sparkling pool, emerald with watercress and lush waterweed.
'In the old days,' he said, 'this water had no equal.'
'That is fine,' said Patrick, 'now we shall share our food. Give half of it to those great survivors of the *fian* there, they need it.' So they blessed the meat and there was enough for everyone. But Patrick longed to know about Fionn and his times.
'Wasn't Fionn mac Cumhall a good lord to you Caoilte?' he asked.
'Indeed he was,' said Caoilte. 'Were all the bounties of nature turned into pure silver or fine gold, Fionn would have given them all away, such was his generosity.'
'What kept you going through all your long lives?' asked Patrick.
'It was the truth that we held in our hearts,' Caolite answered, 'the truth that we kept in our words and the truth that we showed by our actions.'
'Tell me, Caoilte,' said Patrick wistfully. 'In the houses you used to visit long before our time, were there drinking horns and cups and goblets made of crystal decorated with pale gleaming gold?'
'Noble and holy Patrick,' Caoilte said. 'There were 312 drinking-horns in my lord's house, each filled to the brim with foaming ale.'
'Did you have horses and cavalry in the *fian*?'
'We surely did,' he answered. 'Do you know, we used to get 150 foals from a single mare and one stallion.' He then explained how with a story. Caoilte sat and talked, delighting the holy men with tales about the triumphs and sorrows of Fionn and his men, just as the story-tellers of Gaelic Scotland and the west of Ireland do today, keeping alive the memory of the great ancient people who, perhaps, sleep on still in the *sibh* mounds of Ireland.

The Four Branches of The Mabinogion

The Mabinogion is a superb collection of tales which were written down in medieval Wales. They were created by story-tellers reared in the elegant sophistication of Norman chivalry and courtly behaviour, but occasionally the smooth heraldic surface is disturbed by a disquieting ripple like a smooth stone breaking through the calm waters of a tranquil lake. The benign king, the demure queen, the courtiers and handmaidens reveal characters and perform deeds more in keeping with the darker, less polished world in which they had their origin as gods and goddesses. Druidic magic, animal transformations and rough, earthy humour better suited to the Celtic Iron Age than to their idealized literary world make their appearance. This is especially so in the oldest stories known as 'The Four Branches', where these supernatural elements are to the forefront. It is abundantly clear that, beneath all the additions of later influences, there lurks an archaic mythology whose tales were recited in the feasting halls of pagan kings and chieftains, and in cruder form around the fires of humbler homes. Several of the gods and goddesses of *The Mabinogion* have their counterparts in the wider Celtic world, and by comparing them with evidence from other sources, it is possible delicately to remove the veneer of medieval courtly grandeur and glimpse something of the codes and customs of the pagan Britons.

The first Branch of *The Mabinogion* tells the story of Pwyll. Pwyll, Lord of Dyfed in South Wales, ruled over the seven *cantrefs* (divisions) of Dyfed. One of his chief courts was at Arberth and he was staying there once when he decided to go hunting in the lovely lush woodlands of Glyn Cuch.

He let loose his hunting dogs, sounded his horn to muster the pack and rode swiftly after them into the trees. As he penetrated deeper into the forest he lost his companions and when night fell, he found himself alone. Suddenly he heard the cries of another pack of hounds coming towards his own dogs. In front of him was a clearing in the wood, smooth as a well-tended lawn, and as he reached it, Pwyll saw a fine stag closely pursued by the strange pack who surrounded it, baying, and brought it down.

Pwyll was so amazed at the sight of these dogs that at first he had no eyes for their prey. He had never in his life seen dogs like them, for they were blazing white with bright red ears; clearly, they were Otherworld dogs. However, the fallen stag was too good to miss and he drove off the strange pack and set his own dogs on to it.

Suddenly he became aware of a horseman approaching him on a big, grey, dappled steed, wearing a brownish-grey hunting habit and with a hunting-horn about his neck. The stranger came up to Pwyll and his look was not friendly.

'Lord', he said, 'although I know who you are, I will not greet you properly, because of your boorishness and lack of courtesy.'

'What lack of courtesy have you observed in me, Lord?' asked Pwyll, bewildered.

'I have never seen greater discourtesy in any man,' said the stranger, 'than to drive off dogs that have killed a stag and then to set your own pack on it. Was that not indeed ill-mannered? However, I will not avenge myself on you, but will accept instead the payment of one hundred stags.'

'Lord,' said Pwyll, 'if I have so wronged you I will atone for it in accordance with your rank,'

for in those days retribution was made according to the status of the injured party. 'But I do not know who you are.'

'I am Arawn, King of Annwn,' said the stranger and Pwyll looked grave for he knew that Annwn was the Otherworld.

'Lord,' said Pwyll, 'how then may I make amends?'

'I'll tell you,' replied the king. 'There is a king named Hafgan whose kingdom borders mine in Annwn. He is always attacking my land. I cannot defeat him but you could do it easily. If you succeed you will gain my friendship.'

'I will do it,' replied Pwyll, 'but you must tell me how.'

'Listen carefully,' said Arawn. 'I will make a strong pact of friendship with you and transform you into my exact likeness so that everyone will think you are me. Then I will put you in Annwn in my place and every night the fairest woman in the world will be your bed-mate. Remain there in Annwn for a year and a day and then meet with me here once more. A year from this night I have an assignation with Hafgan at the ford. Be there in my likeness and strike him with a single blow—there will be no

need for more. And even though he begs you to strike him again, for pity's sake, on no account do so or he will regain all his strength and vigour. No matter what I might do to him, he would be recovered and ready to fight me again next day, but you will overcome him easily.'
'But what about my own kingdom?' asked Pwyll.
'I will go there myself, transformed into your likeness and I shall reign there in your place.'
'Then I agree,' said Pwyll.

The transformation took place and Arawn accompanied Pwyll until they came in sight of his royal court in the kingdom of Annwn. 'Now,' said Arawn, 'the court and the whole kingdom are your subjects. Go in without fear. If you do as you see others doing, you will soon learn the manners of my court.'

Pwyll went on alone, leaving Arawn to return to his own earthly kingdom. No-one in the world could have imagined the marvellous buildings of all kinds he saw around him as he made his way through rich halls and chambers to the great hall. As Arawn had promised, everyone treated him as if he were their king returning from a normal hunting expedition. Squires pulled off his boots and two knights took away his hunting clothes and dressed him in a robe of golden silk brocade. The feasting hall was made ready and Arawn's knights and champions entered, splendidly equipped and handsome. With them was the most beautiful woman in the world, dressed in a gown of bright brocaded silk. They washed and then went to sit at the long tables.

Pwyll and the queen began to talk and her conversation was enchanting—sweet, intelligent, gracious, uncontrived. And so they spent the evening, eating and drinking and making merry with songs and music and tales. Then it was time for sleeping and Pwyll and the lovely queen went to their bed; as soon as they were there, he turned his back on her and spoke never a word until the morning.

Pwyll passed his year in the Otherworld pleasantly enough, hunting and feasting, and seeing to the affairs of the realm. Every night he and the queen lay together in the same bed and every night he turned his back on her and fell asleep. Next day they were always tender and affectionate, but it was the same on the last night they were together as it had been on the first. Then came the night for his encounter with Hafgan. Everyone in the kingdom knew about that and Pwyll went to the ford as arranged, with a great company of Otherworld nobles around him. On the other side, they could see King Hafgan and his men assembled, waiting for them. At once a horsemen rode up. 'Nobles,' he cried, 'this is a single combat between two kings who are in conflict. Stand back and let them fight it out alone.'

The two kings rode out to the middle of the ford, for that is where conflicts were fought between single warriors in Celtic times. Before Hafgan could make his move, Pwyll struck him right in the middle of his shield-boss so that it split in two. The blow was so strong that his armour was shattered and he was flung over his horse's head onto the hard ground, mortally wounded.

Hafgan realized that his attacker was not Arawn and he cried out: 'Lord, what right have you to kill me? I brought no claim against you. But, for the sake of God, since you have begun my death, finish it.'
'Lord,' replied Pwyll, 'I may yet live to regret what I have done to you. Get whomsoever you wish to deal you the final blow. I will not do it.'
'Then take me away, my men,' said Hafgan, 'for my death has been accomplished.'

Pwyll claimed Hafgan's kingdom as his own and by noon on the following day he was the sole and undisputed king of all Annwn.

Having kept his part of the bargain, Pwyll set off to keep his tryst with Arawn in Glyn Cuch. He found the Otherworld king already there waiting for him.
'May God reward you for your friendship, for I have heard what you have done,' said Arawn.
'Indeed,' said Pwyll, 'when you return to your country you will see what I have done for you.'

Then each took on his proper likeness once more and Arawn set off for his own country. He was overjoyed to see his court and his warriors but they, of course, knew nothing of his long absence, so felt no novelty in his arrival. That day he feasted and laughed and

talked eagerly with his beautiful wife. When the time for sleep came, they went to bed and were loving one with the other. His wife wondered what had happened to her husband after so long but she said nothing. In the night he woke up and, finding her lying there awake, he spoke to her again but she said nothing; later he woke again, and then a third time but not a single word did she utter.

'Why do you not speak to me?' he asked.

'Why, Lord,' she replied, 'for a whole year I have not dared to speak to you in this bed.'

'But we have lain here together every night,' he said.

'And it is my shame that for the past year from the time we pulled the bed-covers over us until morning we have neither spoken to each other nor have you even turned your face towards me, let alone loved me.'

Arawn was astounded. 'The comrade I found was indeed a good and loyal man,' he thought and he said to his wife, 'Lady, do not blame me. In truth I have not slept with you for a year and a night.' And he explained all that had happened between him and Pwyll.

'You had a good and faithful friend indeed,' she said.

'Lady,' said Arawn, 'I was thinking the very same.'

Pwyll, Lord of Dyfed, also returned to his court and there he asked his nobles how they judged his rule during the past year.

'Lord,' they said, 'never were you more discreet and discerning, never more charming, never so generous with your possessions, never has your rule been better.'

'You would do well to thank the man who has been in my place,' Pwyll said and he told them what had happened.

'Praise God that you have known such friendship,' they said. 'Let us pray that you continue to rule us in the same fashion.'

'That I will,' replied Pwyll.

So a firm bond of friendship was sealed between the two kings and they sent each other presents of horses and hounds and hawks and all the things each thought would delight the other. From that time, because of his stay in the Otherworld kingdom of Annwn and his excellent rule there and because he had through his own valour and courage united the two kingdoms, Pwyll was no longer known as Pwyll, Lord of Dyfed. Instead he was called Pwyll, Head of Annwn and he became Lord of the Otherworld as did his son Pryderi after him. And this was only right for although Pwyll, whose name means 'Wisdom' and his son Pryderi, whose name means 'Care', were treated as mortals by the storyteller, they, like Arawn and Hafgan, were among the gods of pagan Celtic Britain.

Branwen, daughter of Llyr

Bran the Blessed, known in Welsh as Bendigeidfran or Blessed Raven, was another of the powerful gods of pagan Celtic Britain. He, his brother Manawydan and his sister, the beautiful Branwen, were the children of Llyr, the old god of the sea. In this story Bran appears as a human-being, though one of gigantic size, but as the tale unfolds he takes on more and more of his supernatural nature. The events, too, seem to happen in real, identifiable places but the characters move freely into the Otherworld where a year passes as quickly as a minute and gods and men feast together. The strange tale of the severed head that lived on after its owner's death provides us with the most convincing literary evidence for the widespread Celtic worship of the severed head with its many magical powers.

Bran the Blessed was king of the island of Britain and crowned in London. He was staying once at one of his courts, at Harddlech in Wales and one afternoon he and his retinue were sitting on the rocks, looking out at the sea. As they sat there, they saw thirteen ships gliding smoothly over the water towards them from the direction of Ireland.

'I can see ships out there,' said the king, 'and they're making straight for us. Tell the men to arm themselves and find out what they want.'

All the ships had beautiful flags made of embroidered silk, and when one outstripped the rest the watchers saw a shield held high above the deck as a sign that the strangers came in peace. The sailors in the leading ship lowered small boats, rowed to the shore and greeted Bran, who stood on a rock high above their heads.

'God bless you,' he cried, 'and welcome. Whose fleet is this? Do they wish to land?'

'These are the ships of Matholwch, King of Ireland, and he is here with them,' they answered. 'He wants to become your ally, Lord, and has come to ask for the hand of your sister, Branwen, so that Britain and Ireland may be joined and grow stronger together. He will not set foot on your shores unless you grant it.'

'Well,' said Bran, 'we'll have to take counsel on that question. But please land, in any case.'

Bran gave the Irish king a royal welcome and there was a magnificent feast at the court that night. The next day, Bran discussed the matter with his advisers and it was decided to give Branwen to Matholwch in marriage. Another great feast began, held not in a house but in a great pavilion, for Bran was so gigantic there was never a house big enough to contain him. When the time came for bed, Branwen slept with the king of Ireland and so became his wife.

Bran had a half-brother named Efnisien who could never bear to see anything going well between people. The next morning he went to where Matholwch's horses were stabled to see if he could disrupt things.

'Whose horses are these?' he asked arrogantly.

'Those are the steeds of the king of Ireland, Matholwch,' the grooms answered.

'Well, what are they doing here?' he asked.

'Matholwch has slept with your sister, Branwen, and that's why his horses are here.'

Efnisien knew all this already but pretended to fly into a rage.

'They've given my excellent sister to the King of Ireland without first asking my permission, have they?' he shouted. 'No-one could have insulted me more.' He then attacked Matholwch's horses and cut off their lips, ears and tails so that the poor creatures were good for nothing.

Of course, the news soon reached Matholwch.

'This is a great and deliberate insult,' his messengers said. 'You have no choice now but to go to the ships.'

When Bran heard that Matholwch was leaving his court without asking his permission, or even saying farewell, he sent messengers to find out the reason. They caught up with the Irish king and asked him why he was leaving.

'Indeed,' said Matholwch, 'had I known what I know now, I would never have come here in the first place. I have been bitterly insulted. No-one ever went on a less happy errand. And there's one thing I cannot understand. Why should I have been treated so badly after I had been given the beautiful girl, Branwen?'

'Believe us, Lord,' said the messengers, 'it was not with the authority of the king that these

of food from the kitchens and then trained it to talk. When it was quite ready, she sent it flying to her brother with a message about her hardships. Bran was outraged and at once declared war on Matholwch.

Bran's army set out in their ships for Ireland but Bran himself was so enormous that he waded across, carrying all the harpists of the court on his back. The fighting was bitter and almost everyone in Ireland perished. Only seven men from Bran's forces escaped: one of them was Pryderi, son of Pwyll, who was also the Head of Annwn; another was Bran's brother Manawydan. Bran himself was fatally wounded by a poisonous spear and before he died he made a strange request. He demanded that they should cut off his head.

'Now take my head,' he told them, 'and carry it with you to London. When you arrive there, bury it at the White Mount with its face towards France. But much will happen before you reach London and can do as I say. You will spend seven years feasting in Harddlech and the head will be a good host to you, as good as it was when it was on my body. Then you'll spend eighty years in Penfro, and as long as you don't open the door that looks towards Cornwall, you can stay feasting there and the head will not rot. But once you've opened that door, you will be unable to stay there any longer; then you must make for London and bury the head. Now go.'

They cut off Bran's head as he had requested and the seven of them and Branwen sailed from Ireland, carrying the head carefully with them. When they had landed in Britain, Branwen looked back at Ireland and around her at Britain and cried out in anguish, 'Son of God, why was I ever born? These two good islands have been utterly wrecked because of me.' At that moment her heart broke and they buried her on the bank of the River Alaw in Anglesey, where even today there is a place they call *Bedd Branwen*, which means Branwen's grave.

The seven saddened men went on their way towards Harddlech with Bran's head. As they walked they met a group of forlorn people on the road and asked them for news.

'The news is terrible,' the travellers moaned.

dreadful deeds were done. If you take this as an insult, it will be even worse for Bran.'

'I know that,' replied Matholwch, 'but Bran cannot undo what has been done.'

In the end, however, the messengers were able to soothe the angry king. Matholwch was seemingly reconciled with Bran and his council and returned to Ireland with Branwen, loaded with the many treasures Bran gave him as compensation for the insult Efnisien had inflicted on him.

At first all went well for Branwen in Ireland and in due course she gave birth to a son, who was given to the best foster-parents in Ireland. Then rumours began to circulate about the great insult which Matholwch had suffered at the hands of his queen's people; eventually he became a figure of fun and mockery and was given no peace until he took steps to avenge the wrong. Branwen was driven from his bedroom and made a skivvy in the court kitchens, cooking for the whole household. Every day the butcher who came to cut up the meat boxed her ears as part of her punishment. To make sure that Bran did not discover what was happening to his sister, Matholwch's men demanded that he ban all ships, ferry-boats and coracles from sailing between Ireland and Wales.

This situation continued for three years but Branwen was not the kind of woman who suffered ill-treatment meekly. She managed to catch and tame a starling by feeding it on scraps

'Caswallawn, Beli's son, has captured Britain and is now crowned king in London.'
'What has happened to Bran's son and all the rest?' the seven asked.
'They are all dead,' the travellers replied sadly.

The men went on their way to Harddlech and discovered a fine feasting hall where they refreshed their weary bodies and their sorrowful souls with the food and drink they found there. As they rested, three birds belonging to Riannon, Pwyll's wife, came to sing to them. The wonder of their magical singing drowned their sorrows and as they listened, seven years passed as quickly as a day.

After seven years it was time to take Bran's head and go to Penfro. Here again they found a splendid feasting hall with a fine view over the sea. Two of its three doors were open. The third was closed and they knew this must be the door that Bran had warned them about. That night was better than any they had ever spent in their lives, for once inside the hall they forgot their mortal misfortunes and the pressure of grief that lay on them was lifted.

They stayed in the feasting hall for eighty long years but the time passed so swiftly and merrily that it seemed no longer than a few short days. Bran's head presided at the feast better than the king himself had done when alive and forever after the feast was known as 'The Assembly of the Wondrous Head'. But it had to end, of course, as Bran had foreseen, and one day one of the seven said, 'I'm going to try opening that door there, just to see if Bran was right.' Before his companions could stop him, he wrenched it open and there was Cornwall in the far distance. Immediately, each one felt the weight of his loss and his grief and all the desolation that had been forgotten in the delights of the feasting hall at Penfro. They remembered all those who had perished, all their past misfortunes and failures. More than anything, however, they grieved for their king. The only thing left for them to do now was to set out for London.

When they reached the White Mount, they buried the head as Bran had asked and for as long as it lay undisturbed, the head protected the land from plagues and invasion.

Manawydan, son of Llyr

Manawydan, the brother of Bran and Branwen, was one of the seven who survived the battle against Matholwch in Ireland and travelled with his brother's severed head to London. His story is full of supernatural elements and magical situations for like the other leading characters in the story, he was one of the Celtic gods, a sea god like his father. At the time of this tale, Pwyll, Lord of Annwn, has died but his widow, Riannon, is still alive and their son, Pryderi, is now Lord of the Underworld (and Dyfed) in his place. The mood of the story is desolate: the events bewildering and strange.

When the seven men had buried Bran's head at the White Mount in London, as Bran himself had instructed, Manawydan was overcome by a terrible sense of deprivation and grief.
'Oh dear God,' he sighed, 'I have no place to go.'
'Lord,' said Pryderi, 'do not be so downcast. The man who rules in Bran's place is your own cousin Caswallawn. Though he has wronged your family, you yourself were never in line for the throne.'
'I know he is my cousin,' sighed Manawydan, 'but the truth is I am sad to see the country ruled by anyone other than my brother Bran. I could not bear to live in Caswallawn's stronghold.'
'Will you take my advice?' asked Pryderi.
'Indeed, I need it,' replied Manawydan.
'I inherited from my father the seven *cantrefs* of Dyfed, the finest land in all the world. My widowed mother, Riannon, lives there now and I will give you her hand in marriage. Then, although the seven *cantrefs* are really mine, I will bestow them on my mother and you with my blessing.'
'May God repay you, Pryderi,' said Manawydan, 'I will go with you to Dyfed.'

They set out on the long road and when they arrived, Riannon and Pryderi's wife Cigfa prepared a great feast to welcome them. Manawydan and Riannon were soon deep in conversation. As the evening went on, Manawydan became so deeply impressed by Riannon's sharp intellect and by her noble,

mature beauty that he quite fell in love with
her.

'Pryderi,' he said, 'I wish to do as you
suggested.'

'Lady mother,' said Pryderi, 'I have given your
hand to Manawydan, son of Llyr, so that you
may be joined in wedlock.'

'That will please me well,' she said.

'And me,' said Manawydan, 'and may God
reward a man of such staunch friendship.'

That night Manawydan and Riannon slept in
the same bed and she became his wife.

Pryderi and Cigfa, Manawydan and Riannon,
stayed together in the beautiful land of Dyfed,
enjoying each other's company so much that
none wished to be parted from the others by
day or by night. One night they held a great
feast at one of their chief courts, in Arberth.
During the evening, the four slipped away while
the courtiers were still at table and went to sit
on an enchanted mound, Gorsedd Arberth. The
place had a special importance for Riannon for
it was there that Pwyll, Pryderi's father, had
first seen her coming towards him on her slow,

stately, willow-white horse. As they sat there
the soft night was disturbed by a sudden,
frightening crash of thunder and a magical mist
settled on them so that they could not see one
another. When the mist lifted, the world around
them had totally changed: there was nothing
but desolation as far as they could see.

Filled with foreboding they hurried back to
the court. Every building was empty and
deserted, courtiers, servants, dogs and horses
had all disappeared and the feasting hall they
had left full of music and talk was silent and
abandoned. Wondering and afraid, they set out
to search the land but though they travelled
through the whole of Dyfed the only signs of
life they could find were those of wild beasts
and birds.

After two years, Manawydan said: 'In truth,
we cannot go on living like wild hunters for
ever. Let us make for England and learn some
craft to earn our living.'

First, they went to Hereford on the borders
of Dyfed and there they decided to learn the art
of saddle-making. Manawydan made the
pommels and coloured them and his work was
so excellent that no other saddler could rival
him. The local saddlers hated him for this and
plotted to kill him, but the four were warned in
good time and moved on to another city.

'What craft shall we practise here?' asked
Pryderi.

'We will make shields,' answered Manawydan.

The same thing happened as before: so
excellent were the shields they made and so
great the jealousy this aroused that they had to
run for their lives.

'What shall we do now?' asked Manawydan.

'Whatever you wish,' answered Pryderi.

'Shoe-making,' Manawydan said. 'Surely we
shall not annoy anyone in that trade.' But he
was wrong, for once again his work was better
than that of the local craftsmen and trouble
started there as it had everywhere else.

'Let us return to Dyfed,' Manawydan said
finally, 'for there is no place for us here.'

So the four went home to live by hunting for
another year. One day Manawydan and Pryderi
were woken by the barking of their dogs and
followed them into the forest until they came to

a clearing where they saw a magnificent silver-white boar. It ran into the bushes, then reappeared, as if inviting them to pursue it. Curious, they gave chase and followed it to a strange and splendid fort. The boar disappeared inside with the dogs close on its heels and Pryderi and Manawydan stopped to stare at the building, which, though they had roamed every inch of the forest, they had never seen before. 'Lord,' Manawydan said to Pryderi, 'take my advice. Don't go inside. We know nothing about this fort.'

No matter how hard he tried, however, he could not dissuade Pryderi from rescuing his hounds. Inside, Pryderi ran from room to room and found the fort deserted, with no sign of either the boar or his hounds. Then, in the innermost courtyard he saw a fountain enclosed in marble. Beside the fountain there was a golden bowl lying on a marble slab on the ground and attached to four chains which disappeared straight up into the air. Pryderi was enraptured by this magical sight. He stepped forward and put out his hands to take hold of the bowl. As soon as he touched it, his hands stuck fast to it and his feet stuck to the ground where he knelt. When he tried to call out, he found he had quite lost his voice and could utter no sound. He was helpless.

Manawydan waited in vain for Pryderi to return and at dusk he returned alone to the place where they were living.

'Where is Pryderi and where are the hunting dogs?' asked Riannon anxiously.

When he told her, she cried out, 'You have been a bad friend today, and you have lost a good one.' Without another word she ran into the forest and soon found Pryderi stuck fast. 'Oh, my son,' she cried, 'what has happened to you?' and, thinking that she could pull him free, she seized the bowl. Instantly she, too, was held fast and made speechless. When darkness fell, there was a mighty peel of thunder, a dark mist swirled around and the fort disappeared with Riannon and Pryderi still inside it.

Manawydan and Cigfa did not wish to stay in Dyfed, where they had both lost the people they loved most, so they returned to England and began to make shoes again. Once more they were too successful at their craft and after a year they were driven away by jealous rivals. Sadly, they returned to the empty land of Dyfed. This time Manawydan took back with them some wheat seeds and he and Cigfa settled in Arberth where they began to hunt and farm.

There was no finer grain in the world than that which Manawydan grew. Harvest time came and the wheat in his three fields looked splendid, the ripe heads hanging heavy and golden in the sun. However, when the morning came for him to reap his first field, he was startled to discover that the corn-stalks were bare and the ears of wheat were gone. Next day he went to harvest his second field and to his

dismay he found that it, too, had been stripped. 'Whoever has taken my crop twice will surely return,' he thought. 'I will keep watch tonight.'

That night he crouched silently at the edge of the third field and sure enough, towards midnight, he heard a rustling. The next moment the field was invaded by a great army of the biggest mice he had ever seen. They set about the crop and began nibbling off and carrying away the richly ripened ears of wheat. He rushed among them in a fury but the mice were too quick for him and all except one escaped. This mouse was slow and cumbersome and he snatched it up, put it in his glove and tied up the wrist opening.

'What have you got there?' Cigfa asked as Manawydan hung the glove up by the fire.

'A thief,' he answered.

'What sort of thief?' she asked.

'A mouse,' he said, explaining what he had seen. 'And if I could get the others, I'd hang the lot.'

'Lord,' said Cigfa, 'it is not proper for one of your rank to hang a mere mouse. Release her.'

'If there was any reason to take your advice, I'd take it,' he replied angrily, 'but since I don't know of any, I'll hang her.'

Early next morning Manawydan brought the mouse to Gorsedd Arberth, the magic mound where all their troubles had begun. He stuck two twigs in the ground on top of the mound to make a tiny gallows then suddenly noticed a threadbare old clerk walking towards him. This was the first person Manawydan had seen in Dyfed for seven long years, apart from his three companions and he stood up to greet him.

'Good day to you,' he said. 'Where have you come from?'

'From England,' the clerk replied. 'And what, Lord, are you doing there?'

'Hanging a thief,' answered Manawydan.

'That looks like a mouse to me. A man of your rank should not stoop to that. Let it go.'

'That I will not,' answered Manawydan heatedly. The clerk offered to buy the mouse's freedom for a pound in order to save Manawydan's dignity, but Manawydan was adamant and the clerk rode on.

As he was fastening a third stick to make the crossbeam of the gallows, Manawydan saw a priest coming towards him and he, too, asked what Manawydan was doing. Like the clerk, the priest advised Manawydan against such unseemly conduct, and offered to buy the mouse's freedom for three pounds; but Manawydan refused and the priest went away.

Manawydan was slipping the noose over the mouse's head when a bishop arrived with his full retinue. He, too, asked Manawydan not to hang the mouse.

'I will give you all the horses you see there on the plain and the seven great loads they are carrying if you let that mouse go free,' he said.

'I will not free her,' Manawydan said.

'What can I give you then?' asked the bishop.

'Remove the enchantment from Dyfed,' said Manawydan, who knew that this was no ordinary bishop.

'Alright,' replied the bishop, 'so let her go.'

'By God, I swear I will not,' said Manawydan 'until you free my wife Riannon and my step-son Pryderi from the enchantment you have placed on them and until you promise not to harm us again.'

To all this the bishop agreed, but Manawydan still had one more condition to make. 'I must know who that mouse is first.'

'She is my wife,' the bishop told him. 'The mice are my war-band and I have done all this to spite Pryderi. My name is Llwyd and his parents wronged my father long ago; this enchantment is my revenge. But now my wife is with child. Release her and I will do anything you ask of me.'

'I will not free her until I have Riannon and Pryderi safe with me here.'

'Here they are,' said Llwyd and, in an instant Riannon and Pryderi appeared, safe and well.

So Manawydan freed the mouse and Llwyd struck her with his druidic staff: the mouse vanished and in her place stood a lovely girl.

Then Manawydan stood up and looked around and saw that Dyfed was as it used to be, freed from enchantment, a good and beautiful land. So Manawydan was reunited with Riannon and Cigfa was reunited with Pryderi and the people of Dyfed returned to their towns and villages and life went on as it had before.

Math, son of Mathonwy

Math, son of Mathonwy, was lord of Gwynedd in North Wales and he had a peculiar need: except when he was at war, he could not live unless a young virgin was with him to keep his feet warm in her lap. At the time of this story, the girl was Goewin, and she was exceedingly beautiful. Gilfaethwy, one of the king's nephews, fell deeply in love with her and almost wasted away in his despair.

His brother, Gwydion, noticed that something was troubling him and asked him what it was.

'I cannot tell you,' said Gilfaethwy. 'You know that Math can hear the softest whisper.'

'You don't need to say anything, I know it already. Goewin is the trouble.'

Gilfaethwy sighed deeply.

'Sighing won't help you,' said Gwydion, 'but don't worry. I shall arrange everything. If we can send Math out to fight, he will have to leave the girl behind.'

The two brothers went to Math and Gwydion pretended to have some interesting news.

'Lord,' said Gwydion, 'I have heard that strange creatures have come to the south. They say that no-one has ever seen anything like them before and that their meat tastes far better than ox meat.'

'What are they called?' asked Math.

'Pigs,' said Gwydion.

'Whose are they and how can we get them?' Math asked.

'They are Pryderi's,' Gwydion replied. 'They were a present from Arawn, king of Annwn. My plan is for twelve of us to go to his castle disguised as bards and ask for them.'

'Maybe he will refuse you,' Math said.

'I'll make sure he doesn't,' said Gwydion.

Gwydion, Gilfaethwy and ten companions found Pryderi at one of his courts and were invited to sit beside him at the feasting table. When Pryderi asked one of them to tell a tale, Gwydion declared that as chief bard, he would speak himself. Now there was no storyteller in the whole world to equal Gwydion and he held the court entranced tales for the whole evening.

At last his tales came to an end and he turned to Pryderi.

'Lord, I would ask a favour of you.'

'What is that?' asked Pryderi.

'I would like to have those animals which Arawn sent you.'

'I would certainly give them to you,' Pryderi answered, 'but I promised Arawn that I would neither give them away nor sell them until they have bred twice their number here.'

'I can deal with that,' said Gwydion. 'Don't give them to me tonight, but don't refuse them either. Tomorrow I shall show you how to free yourself from your promise.'

The twelve young men went to their sleeping-quarters to discuss the matter. Since Pryderi would not part with gifts from the Otherworld easily, Gwydion decided to use his magic powers to trick him. Weaving his spells over a cluster of toadstools, he created twelve stallions with golden saddles and bridles, twelve black and white dogs with golden collars and leashes and twelve golden shields. The next day he went back to Pryderi.

'I know how you can get out of your promise to Arawn,' he said. 'Instead of selling or giving away the pigs, you can exchange them for something much better. I will give you these fine horses with their golden saddles and bridles; these dogs with golden collars and leashes and twelve golden shields as well.'

Pryderi agreed at once, Gwydion took charge of the pigs and the twelve young men set out for the north. They travelled as quickly as they could, for they knew that Gwydion's magic animals would vanish after twenty-four hours and that Pryderi would come raging after them. By the time they reached Gwynedd and had herded the pigs safely into a sty, Math was already marching out to meet an army of angry southerners.

Gwydion and Gilfaethwy pretended to set out to join Math but that night they crept back to Math's castle. Gwydion's plans had all succeeded and the two brothers forced the virgin Goewin to sleep with Gylfaethwy in Math's own bed.

The next day the two brothers joined Math's army and the battle began. Many died on both

sides before Pryderi's army was forced to give way and Pryderi challenged Gwydion, the cause of all the trouble, to single combat. Both men agreed that this would end the quarrel and in the fierce fight that followed, Pryderi was killed, defeated by Gwydion's superior strength and magic powers.

The men from the south were bitter: they had lost their lord, many of their nobles and countless horses and weapons. The men from the north were triumphant and Math returned victorious to his castle while Gwydion, Gilfaethwy and their war-band set off to ride around the boundaries of Gwynedd as was customary after an exploit of this kind.

When Math arrived home and called Goewin to take his feet in her lap, she came to him in a state of deep shame.

'Lord,' she said, 'find another maiden to be your servant. To my shame, I am now a woman.'

'How can that be?' asked Math.

'I was raped, Lord,' she said, 'and not quietly either. Everyone in the court heard the uproar. Your own nephews did it. Gwydion brought his brother to your chamber and Gilfaethwy forced himself on me in your own bed.'

'I shall do what I can for you, Goewin,' said Math sadly. 'First I shall seek compensation for your dishonour. Then I will take my own revenge. But you shall be my wedded wife and I shall give you all the power of my kingdom.'

The two brothers were still away making their circuit of the land so Math ordered the people not to provide them with either food or drink. Before long they had to return to court.

'Good day to you, Lord,' they said bravely, but they were ill at ease.

'Have you come to take your punishment then?' Math asked coldly.

'We are in your hands, Lord,' they said.

'I cannot forgive you for all the wrongs you have done me; for my shame and for the death of Pryderi. But since you have submitted to me, I shall begin your punishment.' Seizing his druidic wand he struck Gilfaethwy and changed him into a well-grown hind. Gwydion tried to escape but Math struck him, too and turned him into a stag.

'Now, go and mate and breed and live like animals. Be back here a year from now.'

A year passed and one day Math heard the sounds of his dogs barking wildly in the courtyard. There stood a fine stag and a hind with a well-grown fawn beside them. Math struck the stag and the hind with his druidic wand and, turning them into wild pigs, sent them off again into the forest. But he changed the fawn into a boy and had him baptized, calling him Little Stag. Another year passed and again the dogs caused a commotion in the courtyard. This time they found a wild boar and a sow with a splendid piglet. Once more Math used his druidic wand, changing the young pig into a boy and the boar and sow into a pair of wolves. A year later they returned with a fine cub and Math changed them all into human form.

'Well,' he said, 'you have wronged me, but the disgrace of bearing young from each other is adequate punishment. Men, prepare baths for these two, wash their hair and put fitting apparel on them.'

When the brothers were fully restored, Math received them back into his company. The first thing he asked them was who they thought should replace Goewin.

'Arianrhod, the daughter of your own sister,' Gwydion said at once. Math sent for her and asked her if she was a virgin. The girl was very offended by the question.

'As far as I know I am,' she said.

Math seized his druidic staff and bent it. 'Now step across this,' he commanded, 'and I'll know soon enough if you are a virgin or not.'

Arianrhod stepped over the staff and as she did so, a fine boy with bright yellow hair fell from her womb. Arianrhod fled in shame from the chamber but at the door she gave birth to something else. Before anyone could see what it was, Gwydion had wrapped it in a silken sheet, run to his room and hidden it in a small casket beside his bed. Math arranged for the yellow-haired baby boy to be baptized and cared for and the strange incident was forgotten. Next morning, however, Gwydion was woken by a faint cry from the casket by his bed and when he opened it he saw a tiny child lying there.

The little boy in the casket was brought up by a foster-mother in the town but he often visited the court and Gwydion loved him like his own son. Arianrhod, his mother, disowned him and would never see him. The boy grew quickly and by the time he was four years old he was as tall as a boy of eight. One day Gwydion and the boy walked over to Arianrhod's castle. She welcomed them and asked whose child the boy was.

'Yours,' Gwydion answered.

'What is his name?' Arianrhod asked sharply.

'He doesn't have one yet,' said Gwydion.

'Well then,' Arianrhod answered. 'I vow that he shall never get a name unless he gets it from me. And I won't give him one.'

'You are a wicked woman,' Gwydion shouted. 'You are being spiteful to the boy because his birth shamed you. But the lad shall have a name in spite of you.' He took the boy away in a rage.

The Celts believed that a person's name should describe him or some significant event concerning him - but that the name must be mentioned first as a chance remark. Gwydion knew that Arianrhod would be too wary to fall for any ordinary trick, so he decided to use his magic powers to deceive her. Next day, Gwydion and the boy disguised themselves as shoemakers and went to the shore near Arianrhod's castle. There Gwydion conjured up a ship out of seaweed and they sat on board and began to make beautiful shoes. When Arianrhod heard about it, she sent for some of the shoes but when she tried them on, they did not fit. Even when she sent the exact measurements of her feet, the shoes that were brought were always the wrong size. Finally, she went herself to the ship to be fitted.

Their disguises were so good that Arianrhod did not recognize them and she sat with them on the deck, talking as if they were strangers. Just then, a wren settled on the rails. The boy aimed an arrow at it and hit it. Arianrhod laughed.

'My goodness,' she said, 'that golden-haired lad has a skilful hand.'

'That's right,' said Gwydion triumphantly. 'Now you've given him his name: Lleu Llaw Gyffes, the Shining One of the Skilful Hand.'

At once the fine ship—and all the beautiful shoes—vanished into seaweed and Gwydion and Lleu were themselves again.

'He may have a name now,' Arianrhod said, furious that she had been deceived, 'but I swear he will never take arms unless I provide them for him myself. And I won't.'

Some weeks later, two bards called on Arianrhod's castle and asked to entertain her. She welcomed them gladly and feasting, singing and storytelling continued far into the night. The next morning Arianrhod was woken by the shouts and bustle of a large and hostile army. Rushing to the window, she saw that her castle was surrounded by warriors and that a fleet of ships filled the bay. She ran to the bards in fright and asked what she should do.

'Give us weapons,' the older bard said, 'and we'll try to fight them off.' Quickly, Arianrhod's servants armed the older man while she gave weapons to the younger one herself. As she handed him his sword and shield, the noise faded away and the ships and armies disappeared. The two bards changed into Gwydion and Lleu and Arianrhod realized that she had been tricked by an illusion once again: against her wishes, she had made Lleu into a fully armed warrior.

Arianrhod was more furious than ever. 'I swear,' she said, 'that although he has a name and weapons, he shall never have a human wife.'

'You've always been a vicious woman,' said Gwydion, 'but he'll have a wife in spite of you.'

This time Gwydion asked Math for help. 'I will conjure up a wife for him from flowers,' said Math, and so he did. He took flowers from the oak tree, from the broom and from the meadow-sweet and with them he created the most lovely girl mortal eyes had ever seen. They called her Blodeuedd, or Flower-Face.

As soon as Lleu was old enough to marry, he took her as his wife and so Arianrhod was outwitted once again. With the help of Gwydion and Math, Lleu of the Skilful Hand settled in his own castle in the hills with his wife and there he ruled his land for many years.

The story of Lleu does not end there, however, for evil and deception destroyed his love and almost took his life. It was only after suffering and revenge that he came at last to take his rightful place as Lord of Gwynedd.

The legend of King Arthur

To most people Arthur is the ideal hero, a human with almost supernatural powers, a brave warrior, a tender lover, a wise law-maker and a just king. Did he really exist? Was he, as many people think, a Celtic chieftain in sixth century Britain with a company of warriors at Cadbury Castle? Or was he a pagan Celtic god? Many scholars have spent a lifetime trying to unravel the mysteries of Arthur and although he is best known from the tales of mediaeval poets, he certainly comes from much earlier times: as early as 600 AD his valour was so legendary that none could compare with it. The most likely explanation is that Arthur was a combination of at least two characters: a pagan god named Artor or Artaios in Gaul and an obscure sixth-century Celtic war-leader. There is no historical evidence that he was ever king of the Island of Britain.

With so little actual knowledge of him, it is strange that of all the characters of Celtic history and mythology, it is Arthur who reigns supreme. The historian Geoffrey of Monmouth was the first to turn Arthur from a pagan warrior into a romantic hero. He wrote his *History of the Kings of Britain* in the 1160s and using the legends of his time and inventing a great deal, he made Arthur the son of Uther Pendragon and Igraine, wife of the Duke of Cornwall. In their time, Saxon invaders were pressing the Celtic peoples of Britain hard, for when the Romans withdrew their garrisons in the fifth century Britain was left virtually defenceless. However, the Britons defended themselves courageously, and when, according to Geoffrey, Arthur had been crowned at the age of fifteen he rallied the people to fight the Saxons. His final victory, at Mons Badonicus (perhaps Badbury or Bath), brought peace to Britain for some thirty years.

Geoffrey spread the legend to Europe where it gained considerable political importance, stressing the nobility of the kings of Britain's past. Around the same time, in 1155, the poet Robert Wace produced the story of the Round Table whose shape meant that no-one who sat there could claim to be at its head. The 'Round Table' is now in Winchester Castle but it has recently been dated by scientific methods and we know it was made in mediaeval times, long after Arthur and his knights had vanished from the world.

In the twelfth century Chrétien de Troyes, a French poet, added many other tales to the growing collection of literature about Arthur and his knights and in 1485 Sir Thomas Malory translated many of them into English.

Arthur's name was known all over Europe, from Italy to the north of Scotland and is found in countless place-names and landscape features, especially in the west and south-west of Britain and in Brittany. He is still a magic, legendary figure and tales are still told about him. He is believed to be sleeping with his men in numerous places, for example under Mount Snowdon in Wales, and even under Mount Etna in Sicily.

A place with very strong associations with Arthur is undoubtedly Glastonbury which rises like a magic island above the marshy lowlands of Somerset. Its dramatic tor can be seen for many miles and it is not surprising that it was thought to be the site of Avallon, or Apple Island, the Celtic Otherworld of Arthur's time. In the twelfth century the bones of a tall man and woman were found in the cemetery there and the monks believed these were the remains of Arthur and his queen. They said, too, that in the same grave there was a cross of lead on which was inscribed the words: 'Hic iacet sepultus inclytus rex arturius in insula avalonia': Here in the island of Avallon the famous King Arthur lies buried.

There is still enchantment about Glastonbury and the spirits of Arthur and his knights are never far away from it.

The birth of Arthur

In the days when Uther Pendragon was king of all England, the powerful Duke of Tintagel in Cornwall rebelled against him. After a long series of battles King Uther suggested a truce and the Duke and his wife Igraine travelled to the king's palace to be reconciled with him.

King Uther fell in love with Igraine the moment he saw her but she refused to listen to him and spoke instead to her husband. 'It seems that we were brought here so that I

should be dishonoured' she said. 'We must leave at once. If we ride all night we shall be safely in our own castle by dawn tomorrow.'

Silently they fled from the palace before the king and his courtiers realized what was happening. When Uther discovered what had happened he was furious and sent messengers to summon them back, threatening that if they did not return, it would mean war. Instead of obeying Uther, the duke immediately prepared his Castle Tintagel for war and, leaving his wife safely there, moved with his warriors to another stronghold, Castle Terrabil.

Uther set out with his knights and his warriors and set up his pavilions outside Castle Terrabil, prepared to lay siege to them until the duke would be forced to surrender. Every day the duke's warriors marched out from the castle to fight against King Uther's men and many were killed and wounded on both sides in the

bitter battles. Still the duke showed no sign of defeat and as the days passed, Uther's love for Igraine grew so strong that he fell ill.

'I am so sick with anger and with love for Igraine that nothing will make me whole,' he told his knights.

Now it happened that a powerful wizard named Merlin lived in those times and Uther's men decided he was the only person who could cure the king. A knight was sent to find him and one evening met an old beggar man in the forest.

'Whom do you seek?' asked the beggar.

'That's none of your business,' said the knight.

'Well I know who you are looking for,' said the beggar. 'You are looking for Merlin, and I am he. If King Uther will reward me well and promise to give me what I ask, then I will give him his heart's desire.'

'The king will not refuse you anything that is reasonable,' promised the knight and Merlin told him to ride back with the news.

'I will not be far behind you,' he said.

The knight rode as swiftly as he could but by the time he arrived with his message, Merlin was already there waiting for him. Together they went to King Uther.

'I know everything that is in your heart,' said Merlin 'and if you swear on your honour as a king to do what I ask, you shall have all that you wish for.'

'I agree,' said the king and swore to it upon the Bible.

'Now this is what I ask,' said Merlin. 'On the first night you lie with Igraine, a child will be conceived. When it is born, you will give it to me to rear and it will be good both for your honour and for the child itself.'

'It shall be as you say,' said the king.

'Now prepare yourself for this very night you shall be with Igraine in the castle at Tintagel. You will have the likeness of the duke her husband and I will be with you, in the shape of one of his men. But speak as little as possible while you are there. Say that you are ill and do not stir from your bed until I come to you in the morning.'

Immediately, the king rode off from his pavilion outside Castle Terrabil and set out for Tintagel. The duke, however, was watching from the battlements and he decided that this was a good moment to attack. As night fell, he and his warriors charged out of the gates. A fierce skirmish took place and the duke was killed and his forces defeated.

No more than three hours later, King Uther arrived at Castle Terrabil in the shape of the dead duke and was welcomed in. That night he slept with Igraine and, saying little, left early the next morning as Merlin had instructed him. It was only when a messenger came with the news that the duke had been killed the night before that Igraine realized her bedfellow had been a stranger; wondering and grieving privately, she said nothing about what had happened.

Peace was made between the two armies and Uther proposed marriage to Igraine. On the advice of her counsellors she accepted him and they were married with great celebrations soon afterwards.

It quickly became obvious that Igraine was going to have a child and one night as they lay in bed together, King Uther asked her whose child it would be. Too ashamed to answer, Igraine said nothing.

'Don't be afraid,' said Uther, 'but tell me the truth and I shall love you more than ever.'

Then Igraine told him all that had happened on the night her husband had died and Uther explained that he had been her mysterious visitor and was the father of her child. He explained his pact with Merlin and how it had been arranged for the child to be brought up by a knight named Ector, who would look after it as if it were his own.

In due time Igraine gave birth to a son. Merlin had given Uther instructions about what to do and as soon as the child was born, he was wrapped carefully in a cloth of gold and handed secretly to Merlin who came to the gate of the castle, again disguised as a poor man. Merlin took the baby to Sir Ector and his wife and there the child was christened Arthur and brought up as their own son.

Within a few years, Uther fell seriously ill. For three days and nights he lay unable to speak and it was obvious that his death was near.

Then Merlin came to the knights and barons and told them: 'There is no cure for this sickness and God will have his will. Let all you nobles and knights gather here before the king tomorrow and I will make him speak. Then you shall hear whom he names to be his heir and successor.'

Next day everyone came to the room where King Uther lay and Merlin stood before him and called out: 'Sire, shall your son Arthur be king of all this realm after you?'

Uther turned slowly to face Merlin and his knights and said softly, 'I give him my blessing and name him king hereafter.'

With that he died, and Queen Igraine and his knights mourned for him.

The sword in the stone

All this time Arthur had been living with the knight Ector for although Uther had named an heir to his kingdom, no-one knew who or where he was. After King Uther's death, many powerful lords thought that they should be king, and civil war seemed to be inevitable. To prevent it, Merlin advised the Archbishop of Canterbury to invite all the lords and knights of the land to come to London at Christmas. A miracle, he said, would reveal the rightful king.

All the most important men in the kingdom obeyed the archbishop's summons and on Christmas morning they went into church to pray. When they left the church after the service, they saw that a great marble stone had appeared in the churchyard. In the middle of the stone was a steel anvil and in it was a naked sword, pushed into the anvil up to the hilt. Around the sword were inscribed the words: *'Whoever pulls this sword out of this stone and anvil is the rightful king of all England.'*

Of course all the strongest knights tried to remove the sword but however hard they pulled and tugged at it, it remained stuck fast. 'The true king is not yet here,' the archbishop said 'but God will make him known. Let ten good men guard this sword until he comes.'

After deliberation, it was decided that every

day the lords and their knights of the kingdom should take their turn and try to free the sword. To make sure that the company stayed together until the true king appeared, it was decided to hold a great tournament of jousting on New Year's Day.

News of the miraculous sword and of the tournament spread far and wide and one of the knights who rode to London to join in was Sir Ector. With him came Arthur and Ector's own son Cei. Cei had been made knight only two months before, on All Saints Day, and Arthur was his squire. This was to be Cei's first tournament but as they rode towards the jousting field, he realized he had left his sword behind at their lodgings.

'Ride swiftly and bring me my sword, Arthur,' he said.

'At once,' Arthur said and rode off to find it. When he arrived he found that the house was locked up since everyone had gone to watch the tournament.

'Cei shall not be without a sword today of all days,' he swore to himself. 'I shall ride to the church and bring him the sword from the stone.'

The churchyard was deserted when he arrived, for the guardians of the sword were, like everyone else, at the jousting field. Taking hold of the sword by its hilt, Arthur pulled it out of the anvil as easily as a knife comes through butter and rode back with it to his brother.

Cei recognized the sword immediately and took it to his father.

'Here is the sword from the stone, sire. So I must be king of this land.'

When Sir Ector saw the weapon, he left the tournament and immediately rode back to the deserted churchyard. He strode into the church, took a bible and made Cei swear on it how he had acquired the sword.

'Father,' Cei said, 'Arthur gave it to me.'

'And how did you get it?' Sir Ector asked Arthur, and the boy told him what had happened.

'Were any of the guardians here?' Sir Ector asked.

'No,' said Arthur after a moment's thought.

'Now I understand that you must be king of this land.'

'Why me?' asked Arthur, puzzled.

'It is God's will. No-one except the rightful king can remove this sword from the stone. Now let me see whether you can replace the sword as it was and pull it out again.'

'That's simple,' said Arthur and he put the sword back in the anvil.

First Sir Ector tested the sword himself, then he told Cei to try. But though Cei pulled at the weapon with all his strength, it moved not an inch.

'Now you try,' Sir Ector said to Arthur.

'It's simple enough,' Arthur replied and again he pulled the sword effortlessly out of the stone.

Then Ector and Cei bowed down and kneeled before Arthur to pay him homage.

'Why do you, my own father and brother kneel to me?' cried Arthur.

Then for the first time, Sir Ector told Arthur all that he knew of Arthur's birth, of his secret arrival and of the part Merlin had played.

Arthur was sad because he had believed that

Sir Ector was his true father, but the love between all three was as strong as ever.

They went first to the archbishop to explain what had happened and he decreed that twelve days later all the knights should assemble once more at the stone to prove Arthur's claim before them all. Again everyone tried to extract the sword but only Arthur could remove it. The jealous knights, however, remained unconvinced and demanded another trial and then another, aggrieved that an unknown youth should come to rule over them. After the third trial the people cried out their support for Arthur and at last both rich and poor kneeled before him and acknowledged him as their king. Only then did Merlin reveal to the assembled crowd that Arthur's true father had been their beloved King Uther Pendragon.

Arthur took the sword between his hands and offered it upon the altar, swearing to be a true king, to stand for truth and justice all the days of his life. And in a single day the archbishop first made Arthur a knight and then crowned him king, and he ruled the land wisely and well from that day on.

The sword Excalibur

Immediately Arthur became king of Britain, he set off to explore his realm with only the magician Merlin as his companion. They travelled far and wide and had many dangerous adventures together. On their travels Arthur was badly wounded in a duel with a knight called Pellinore, who had vowed to challenge anyone who came on his land. Pellinore was fierce and strong and would have killed Arthur if Merlin had not cast a spell on him and sent him into a deep slumber.
'What have you done?' cried Arthur. 'You have killed a good man with your magic.'
'Do not worry, for he is wholer than you are and will wake within the hour,' said Merlin. 'He would have killed you if I had not been here but after this he will do you good service.'

Then Merlin took Arthur to a hermit who was a skilled healer and in three days his wounds were cured. As they rode away, Arthur realized that he had lost his sword.
'That is no problem,' said Merlin. 'There is one nearby which shall be yours.'

After a time they came to a broad, clear lake. Rising from the middle of the water was a white-clad arm holding a magnificent sword.
'There,' said Merlin, 'is the sword that I promised you.' As he spoke, they saw a beautiful woman emerge from the water.
'That is the Lady of the Lake,' said Merlin. 'There is a great rock in the lake and within the rock she has a beautiful palace under the water. When she comes to you, speak courteously to her and she will give you the sword.'

The woman walked slowly towards them and Arthur greeted her politely.
'Lady,' he said, 'what is the sword that is held up out of the water? I wish it were mine, for I have no sword of my own.'
'Arthur,' she answered, 'it is the sword Excalibur and it is mine. But if you give me a gift when I ask you, then you shall have it.
'My lady,' Arthur said, 'I shall give you anything you wish.
'Then go to that boat and row out to the sword. Take it and the scabbard and I will come in due course to ask you for my gift.'

The two men tied their horses to a tree and rowed out to the sword. Arthur took hold of it by the hilt and as the hand that held it loosened its grip, both hand and arm disappeared below the surface of the water. Arthur examined it eagerly, wondering at the fine workmanship of the sword.

'Which do you prefer, the sword or the scabbard?' asked Merlin.

'The sword, undoubtedly,' replied Arthur.

'Then you are unwise,' said Merlin, 'for the scabbard has magic powers. While it is with you, you will never be badly wounded. Eventually it will be taken from you but until then keep it always at your side.'

Armed with Excalibur, King Arthur and Merlin rode off into the forest.

The round table

When King Arthur married his wife Guinevere she brought with her as part of her dowry a fine round wooden table, so large that one hundred and fifty knights could sit there at the same time. Its shape meant that no-one was able to take precedence over anyone else and King Arthur and his company of knights became famous not only for their adventures but for the justice and honesty of their lives.

The knights of the round table were the bravest knights in Christendom. Many famous warriors were found in that company including Sir Bedivere, Sir Lancelot and his son Sir Galahad; Sir Gawain the king's nephew, and Sir Tristram of Lionesse. Among them was a young knight named Cynon, a courageous but inexperienced warrior whose story is told here.

One day King Arthur was sitting in his bed-chamber at his court in Caerleon with his men and his wife Guinevere. Sleepily he stretched out on his bed of fresh rushes and bright silk and said, 'Do not laugh at me, men, but I am going to doze off here until my dinner is ready. You can amuse yourselves by telling each other stories and my chief warrior Cei will bring you meat and drink.' He then fell asleep and Cei brought mead and spit-roasted chops.

'Now,' he said, 'as payment for that, I want a story.'

The company decided that the young knight Cynon should tell them the most wonderful thing that had ever happened to him. This is the story he told.

'I was the only son of my parents and I was reckless and conceited. I thought there was nothing I could not do. So when I had travelled up and down this land, I went into the far corners of the world seeking adventure. I eventually came to the most beautiful valley anyone has ever seen, lined with great trees and a river with a path beside it. In the far distance there was a great castle and I set out to ride there. When I arrived I found a golden-haired man waiting for me. He wore a tunic and cloak of yellow-brocaded silk threaded with gold ribbons, and his shoes were fastened with gold. He was the most courteous man in the world, and we went into the castle together.

At first the whole castle seemed deserted but when we came to the great hall we found twenty-four girls sitting sewing silk. They were all so incredibly beautiful that, if you will forgive me, my lady, even the plainest of them by far exceeded Guinevere. They tended my horse, gave me rich garments to wear and placed cushions round me for comfort. When we ate, I was amazed at the splendour of the vessels and had never before tasted such food and drink.

Until we were halfway through the meal there was silence. Then my host decided I was ready to talk and he asked me who I was and where I was going. I boasted that I was looking for someone who could be a fitting rival for me and he smiled gently and said, 'If I wasn't afraid that terrible harm would come to you, I could tell you whom you should meet.' I felt sad when he said this and he could see my dejection.

'Very well,' he said, 'if you prefer to risk great danger, I shall tell you what to do. Tomorrow morning take the same road that led you here. When you come to the forest again, you will find a track on your right. Take it and eventually you will see a large clearing in the trees with a mound in the middle of it. On that you will see an enormous, dark man as big as two human men. He has only one foot, only one arm and a single great eye in the centre of his forehead. In one hand he carries an iron club which two strong men could hardly lift. He is a rude and ugly man, but he is kindly just the same. He is the guardian of the forest and lord of all the animals there. You will see a thousand wild animals grazing about him. Ask him to point out your road to you. Although he will be rude to you, he will tell you where you wish to go.'

I have never known a night to drag on as that one did. When dawn finally came, I rode to the clearing and when I reached it I was amazed. There must have been three thousand animals there. The dark man on the mound was very much bigger than the stranger had warned me and I am sure that it would take four fine warriors to raise his iron club. I greeted him politely yet everything he said to me was offensive and discourteous. Then I asked him to show me what power he had over all these wild creatures.

'I'll show you, little fellow,' he replied. He raised his great club and struck a stag with a fearful blow so that it gave out a belling roar, and all the animals came rushing to the mound. They were as numerous as the stars in the heavens and there was scarcely room for me to stand there. Then all the animals bowed down their heads and paid him homage as servants do to their lord. With a sneer he said, 'Now do you understand my power over them, little man?'

I asked him to direct me on my way and he was gruff and insulting, but he did tell me what I wanted to know.'

'Take the path to the end of the clearing', he said, 'and climb up the slope until you reach the summit. There you will see a great, green valley, and a huge bright green tree in the middle of it. Under the tree is a fountain and beside the fountain a slab of marble and on it is a silver cup fastened to a silver chain. Take it up and throw a bowlful of fountain water on the slab. First there will be a great crash of thunder so that the whole earth will seem to tremble with it. Next there will be a shower so cold that it

will be hard for you to survive it; then there will be a storm of hailstones; and then all will be bright and beautiful. By this time not a single leaf will remain on that tree. Soon a flock of birds will alight on it and no birds of this world can sing like them: they will quite enchant you. Suddenly you will hear panting and loud moaning and you will see a black knight on a pure black horse coming towards you. He will attack you, and there is no way you can escape him. But if you stand your ground, he will soon unhorse you.'

All these things came about, but once again they were much worse than I had expected. The man on the black horse appeared and said, 'Knight what do you want of me? What harm have I done to you that made you damage my realms today?' I attacked him then, Cei, but he soon had me on the ground. He went off leading my horse with him and I had to walk all the way back to the huge, dark man. I can't begin to tell you how he mocked me, Cei; I nearly melted away for shame and humiliation.

Back I went to the castle and there I was made even more welcome than on the previous night. No-one asked me about my day and I told them nothing myself. When I arose in the morning there was a splendid brown-black horse with a bright red mane waiting for me, ready saddled. So I armed myself, blessed my kind hosts and came home. That same horse is

still with me and I wouldn't exchange him for the finest steed in Britain.

'And no man, Cei, ever told such a story against himself as that,' Cynon ended. 'There, you've had your story, as you wished.'

Of all the adventures of the knights of the round table, the most famous was the quest for the Holy Grail—the cup which was used at the Last Supper given by Jesus for his disciples.

Even in King Arthur's time there were many legends about the holy cup, which was said to have been filled with the blood of Jesus by Joseph of Arimathea. But no-one, of course, knew what had happened to it.

One night when King Arthur and his knights were seated at the round table after supper, they heard a great cracking noise of thunder, with a roar so loud it seemed to shake the whole house. In the middle of the blast, a sudden shaft of sunlight streamed into the room, a beam seven times stronger than any normal light. As they looked at one another each thought the others looked more beautiful than ever before and they stared speechless, sure that the hour of doom had come.

As they watched, invisible bearers carried a cup shrouded in white silk through the hall. A smell of overpowering sweetness followed it and on the table before them appeared all the food and drink each one loved best. Silently the cup moved through the room, then vanished as suddenly as it had appeared.

For a while they all sat in awe-struck silence. Then the king thanked God for sending them the vision.

'Certainly,' said Sir Gawain, 'we have been offered a vision of grace. But one thing I vow. Tomorrow and no later, I shall set out in search of the Grail. I long to see it free from its covering and shall continue for as long as possible to look for it. And if I do not find it, I know that I will have been found unworthy to do so.'

When the other knights heard Sir Gawain's vow, they stood up and made the same pledge, but King Arthur was greatly saddened.

'Alas,' he said to Sir Gawain, 'you have nearly killed me with your vow, for you have caused me to lose the fairest fellowship and truest knights that were ever seen. When they leave here, I am sure that many of us will never meet again, because many will die in the quest. I have loved you all as well as my own life and it grieves me to see you go.' Tears filled his eyes, and all the court was troubled.

The vision led to a long and difficult quest through trials and adventures which defeated almost all the famous knights. In the end only Sir Galahad, the young son of Lancelot, was worthy to succeed and even he was not destined to live to bring the news to Arthur in his court.

Some say the Holy Grail lies buried still in the Chalice Well at Glastonbury in Somerset—but that is another story.

The death of Arthur

Arthur's kingdom prospered under his rule. He repulsed the Saxon invaders and conquered many lands. But unknown to him his queen Guinevere and his bravest knight Sir Lancelot secretly loved each other. Eventually their love was discovered and Arthur ordered the arrest of his friend and put his wife on trial for adultery.

Sir Lancelot escaped but Guinevere was condemned to be burned alive. On the appointed day she was tied to the stake, but before the fire could be lit Sir Lancelot led a group of knights to rescue her. Many noble knights on both sides were slain but the couple escaped to Sir Lancelot's castle in France.

Arthur followed to France to win back his wife, leaving his son Mordred in charge of his kingdom. For nearly a year Arthur besieged Sir Lancelot's castle, but the knight still loved his king and tried to avoid battle. Then there came devastating news which forced Arthur and his army to return to Britain. During the king's absence, Mordred had forged letters that said Arthur had been killed in battle. Using these, he had summoned a Parliament and been crowned king. Arthur returned at once to claim him kingdom and a series of bitter battles was fought between father and son. At last the armies were ranged against each other for what everyone knew would be the final conflict.

The night before the battle, Arthur saw a ghost who told him that if he fought his son the next day he would die. To avoid this omen, a truce was arranged and as a sign that the terms were accepted by both sides, King Arthur and Mordred agreed to meet between the two armies. Each would be accompanied by fourteen knights.

As Arthur climbed into the saddle he turned to the ranks of men behind him and told them, 'If you see a drawn sword, come fiercely and kill that traitor, Mordred, because I do not trust him.'

At the same time Mordred told his own men: 'If you see a drawn sword, come to me swiftly and kill anyone who stands in front of you. I do not trust this truce; I know my father wants revenge.'

The parties met in the middle ground between the two armies and made their agreement. Wine was fetched and they were drinking together when an adder crawled out from beneath a bush and bit one of the knights on the foot. Unthinkingly, he drew his sword to kill it and the blade flashed in the sun. At once, both armies roared in anger and charged.

All day the battle raged and at its end a hundred thousand men lay dead upon the ground. Only King Arthur and a few close companions stood alive. In the twilight they could see Mordred leaning on his sword among a great pile of dead men.

'Leave him be,' begged the knights. 'Remember the prophecy of your death; if you do not fight him this wicked day of destiny is past.'

But Arthur ran at Mordred crying, 'Traitor, your death is here.'

When Mordred heard his father's cry, he drew his sword and ran towards him. Arthur plunged his spear deep into his son's body and Mordred, feeling the death wound, plunged forward so that he could reach the king. With his last strength, he cut the king's head open with his sword then fell dead on the ground.

Sadly, King Arthur's last surviving knight carried him from the field.'

Hardly able to speak, Arthur commanded him to take the sword Excalibur to the edge of the lake nearby and cast it in so that it might be returned to its Otherworld owner.

The knight went to obey but when he felt the fine sword in his hand and saw its beautiful ornaments, he longed to possess it and he hid it in the rushes by the lake. When he returned, Arthur asked him what had happened when he threw the sword into the water.
'Nothing,' replied the knight. 'I saw only the lapping of the waves.'

Then Arthur knew that the knight was lying and told him angrily to obey his orders exactly. Again the knight pretended to have done as Arthur asked and again Arthur knew the truth and spoke to him scornfully. Filled with remorse, the knight returned a third time to the lake and this time flung the sword far out into the water.

As he did so, a hand reached out and caught Excalibur, brandishing it three times before disappearing under the waves. The Lady of the Lake had reclaimed her gift. Then the knight lifted Arthur and carried him gently to the shore. There, waiting for them was a barge in which were three queens and their maidservants, all weeping at the sight of the king's terrible wounds. The knight lifted Arthur on board and placed his head in the lap of one of them. The barge rowed slowly away, leaving the knight standing desolate on the shore.
'My lord Arthur, what shall become of me now you go from me and leave me here alone among my enemies?' he cried.
'Comfort yourself,' cried the king, 'and do as well as you can for I am no longer able to help you. I must go to Avallon to be healed of my grievous wounds. And if you never hear of me again, pray for my soul!' With that, the boat disappeared into the mist.

Some say that Arthur lies sleeping still, while his wounds heal and he awaits the call to return to the upper world as its king. Perhaps he lies in Italy far below the fiery mountain of Etna; perhaps at Snowdon in Wales, guarded by two fierce, brave eagles; perhaps at Glastonbury in England, the tall hill which rises like an island of glass, shimmering in a silver haze among the flat lands of Somerset. Wherever he lies, when danger to the country is greatest, Arthur they say, will come again.

The gods of the pagan Celts

In the stories so far, humans and people from the Otherworld of the gods have mingled easily, visiting each other's realms, helping or fighting with one another and sometimes even marrying. This is how they have been remembered in the tales handed down by word of mouth from generation to generation: but what were the old gods of the pagan Celts really like?

Much of what we know about the Celtic gods comes from Roman sources for the Celts did not believe in using writing to record their knowledge. History, genealogy, astronomy, astrology and above all religion were passed down by word of mouth. All knowledge was sacred and the Celts did not wish it to fall into impious hands. They wrote business letters in Greek or Latin but chose to write very little in their own language. This means that many of their most sacred beliefs are only dimly known to us.

The ancient Irish tales contain the earliest written records of Celtic mythology and though they now seem to relate especially to Ireland, the family of gods they involve are probably typical of Celtic tribal beliefs. The Irish gods, who became the 'faery folk of the Otherworld' were known as the Tuatha de Danann, 'people of the goddess Danu'. Danu was considered to be the mother goddess from whom all the others were descended.

Although the gods did not form a simple family of deities like their well organized Greek and Roman equivalents, they did have certain defined areas of influence. Nuada Silver Arm, the king of the gods, was also a warrior god while the goddess known as The Morrigan was a deity of battle; it was important to have her on your side if you hoped to win. The Dagda, the 'good god' was the father god, often shown with a powerful club and a cauldron of plenty. His children included Bodb, Brigid (a goddess of fire and poetry), Ogma (god of literature and strength), Donn (lord of the dead), Angus (god of love). Lir and his son Manannan were gods of the sea; Diancecht and his son Miach were gods of medicine while Goibniu the smith and Credne the metal worker were craftsmen gods. Lugh Long Arm, the all-skilled warrior, was perhaps the most powerful of them all.

The male was important in early Celtic society but the mother or earth goddess seems to have been dominant. She was the divine mother of the tribe and, if properly worshipped, she brought fruitfulness to the land and peace and prosperity to its people. Some male gods were probably originally nature gods, too, but others, including the Dagda, were also worshipped as divine ancestors of the tribe, who had left the human world but still had a great influence over their descendants. The *sidh* mounds where the Otherworld people in Ireland lived after the coming of the Gaels were originally burial mounds.

Because each tribe had its own gods there are literally dozens of named gods and goddesses in the Celtic world, known to us mainly from inscriptions and carvings and from the records of the Romans. Both in the British Isles and in other parts of Europe, the names of gods and goddesses also survive in place and river names. Two important rivers, the River Severn in Britain and the River Seine in France, commemorate respectively the Celtic goddesses Sabrina and Sequana. Both rivers have bores, tidal waves formed by conflict between currents and the tides dominated by the phases of the moon. Even today these bores seem full of a magical energy: to the ancient Celts they represented immense supernatural power. At the source of the Seine, which is located at St-Germain-Source-Seine, a spring head shrine has been excavated; the local museum and the museum at Dijon nearby contain numerous religious objects carved from oak, the tree most sacred to the druids. Sabrina's temple probably stands on a hill at Littledean, Gloucestershire, seven miles north-east of the temple at Lydney dedicated to the god Nuada or Nodons.

Many gods and goddesses of Britain and Gaul seem obscure, especially since it was popular to give the same god several different names. However, archaeologists and linguists now think that some of the gods who appear under one name or another throughout the Celtic world were of greater importance than the more local deities. One of these is Cernunnos, 'the Horned one', the wise, aged but still potent stag-god who, wearing a stag's antlers and brandishing a mysterious ram-headed serpent,

was lord of all animals. Statues from Gaul show him pouring out money from a purse as lord of material prosperity and he was probably also an important ancestor-god. The Dagda, another ancestor-god, had his equivalent in Gaul, Sucellos, 'the Good Striker' who carried a mallet (similar to the Dagda's club) and a dish (similar to the Irish god's cauldron). He is also shown with a dog.

Roman historians identified some Celtic gods with their own: Lugh or Lugos, and a god called Esus were like Mercury; other major gods were Taranis who was also called 'the Thunderer' and Teutates, 'God of the People'. The goddess Brigid was called Bergusia in Gaul and the sinister war-goddesses known in Ireland as the Morrigan were also worshipped in Europe under another name. These war-goddesses were sometimes three people, sometimes one and were especially associated with the raven, a scavenger on every battlefield. Another god shown in carvings from Gaul has a pair of ravens on his shoulders, talking into his ears. Some eight hundred years later, the Vikings worshipped their god Odin, whose two magic ravens rested on his shoulders and each morning flew off to view the world, returning at nightfall to tell their lord and master all that they had seen. Few people know that this Viking god could trace his ancestry far back in the ancient Celtic world.

Another deity associated with animals was the horse goddess, known in Europe as Epona, in Ireland as Macha and in Wales as Riannon. White mares were said to have played an important part in the inauguration of kings, a tradition which links them far back in time and place to ancient Sanskrit rites.

Some of the Celtic gods were destroyed by the coming of Christianity but others were accepted and adapted to become early Christian saints. Brigid or Bergusia was transformed into the evangelizing saint Brigid of Kildare. Danu or Anu, the mother goddess of the Irish family of gods, became Saint Anne, patroness of springs and wells. The names and memories of other gods remain to walk our hills and haunt our valleys; but the god who has retained his magical aura throughout Europe is Lugh, the youthful, all-skilled shining god, the patron of warriors and craftsmen alike.

The story of how Lugh arrived at the sacred palace of Tara was told in the chapter 'The second battle of Moytura' and he appears again as the divine father of Cu Chulainn and as Lleu, the master shoemaker of the Mabinogion. It is interesting that an ancient three-faced stone head found in County Donegal in Ireland was named 'The cobbler' by the local people and the leprechauns of Irish folklore are said to carry on his craft; people still claim they can sometimes hear the quick, light tap-tap-tapping as the leprechauns make shoes for those who believe in them and are generous to them.

The Romans considered Lugh to be the equivalent of their own god Mercury but a description from one of the Irish tales seems to show him as an even more important god, brilliant as the sun itself.

The people of Ireland were preparing to fight against their ancient enemies, the Fomorians, when suddenly a bright light shone out. 'That's strange,' said one. 'The sun is rising in the west today when normally it rises in the east.' 'That is a good sign,' said the druids. 'It is the brilliance of Lugh Long Arm who is coming to help us in the battle.'

Then Lugh appeared before them in all his shining glory and prepared to do battle against the Fomorians. He put on the body-armour of the sea-god Manannan, armour so filled with powerful magic that anyone who wore it was safe from battle wounds. He buckled on Manannan's breast-plate and helmet and, reflected in the gleaming, burnished bronze, his face shone out like the sun itself. Then he swung his glistening, blue-black shield onto his back, slung his smooth, sharp, sword onto the left side of his sword-belt and took his long, poisonous spears in his right hand.

When the men of Ireland saw him they, too, dressed in their battle garments; the pointed spears they raised were like a forest and their shields ranked one beside the other like the stakes of a rampart. And so Lugh set out to protect his people.

Lugh, or Lugos as he was known in Europe, was an important god in Gaul and many towns including Leiden, Laon and Loudon were named after him. One of the most important was Lyon in France, whose old name was Lugudunum, the fortress of Lugh. It was said that Lugh's sacred ravens had appeared at the site and that this had been taken as a favourable omen for building a city there. In Roman times a great festival was held in Lyon in honour of the emperor Augustus. In fact it took over the Celtic god's own feast day, Lughnasa, which was held all over Europe on 1 August. The festival has continued to be celebrated down the ages and is still held today, a surviving, living tribute to this most widely worshipped deity.

Lugh's festival, Lughnasa, and was one of the four great calendar festivals of the Celtic year. The others were Imbolc (1 February), Beltain (1 May) and Samain (1 November). Lughnasa was on 1 August but a whole month was set aside for it, including the last two weeks of July and the first two of August. In Britain Lughnasa was adapted by the Christian faith and became known as Lammas, a first fruit celebration before the harvest. In pagan days, the festival was intended to ensure a good harvest. In those days, disease could destroy an entire year's crop of grain and Lugh was said to fight against an evil god of blight for possession of the harvest.

Saint Columba, the prince-priest who founded the great Celtic church on the island of Iona off western Scotland in the sixth century, actually allowed his monks to continue with their Lughnasa celebration. They were permitted to feast and make merry, and he named that celebration the 'Feast of the Ploughmen'. Many legends are still to be heard and many merry gatherings held, in honour of Lugh's Lammas Feast.

One of these, the Lughnasa fair at Muff Rock in Ireland, takes place in early August and is basically a fair held for the buying and selling of horses. In the old days there were ceremonies around a nearby sacred lake which was thought to have healing powers and a white stallion was probably adorned and set up on the rock. Horse-racing played an important part at these fairs, and horses were swum through the lakes. In times gone by, the battle for the harvest between Lugh and the evil god would have been

acted out. One story about the Lughnasa Fair at Muff Rock is linked with the legend of Fionn, who, it is said, lies sleeping in his burial mound, awaiting the call to save Ireland from danger. The fact that scholars believe Fionn may be another name for the god Lugh makes this especially interesting.

A farmer went to the fair to sell a horse and he agreed with the purchaser to take the animal to his home. They set out together on horseback and, coming to a great mound, were amazed to see it open up before them. They entered a long passage and came to a room in which there were many stalls, each with a horse in it. Beside each horse was an armed warrior; and all were fast asleep.

The farmer, astonished at the sight, bent down to take the sword from the scabbard of one of the sleeping men and he was just reaching out to take hold of it when the warrior

grasped it himself and began to unsheathe it. As the two terrified men fled, they saw the other warriors also stirring to draw their weapons before falling asleep once more.

When they were safely out of the mound, in the open air again, the farmer's companion said, 'It is a shame you did not fully draw the sword. For if you had, all the men and horses would have woken up and come out to save Ireland.'

The memory of the old gods and heroes is still very much alive, especially at the festivals once held in their names.

There are many examples of festivals that originally celebrated Lugh in Ireland and which are still held today. Little research has so far been done on Lughnasa festivals elsewhere, but it is clear that they were common in many of the Celtic or once Celtic countries. The most important evidence comes from Lyon, the town which bore his name.

In 1897, part of a huge bronze calendar for calculating important dates in the Celtic year was discovered by chance at Coligny, 50 miles north-east of Lyon. It was made in the first century AD and clearly shows that Celtic scholars were masters of mathematical calculation. It also shows that a great feast was held in Gaul during the month of Rivros, which means 'great month of the feast', and fell at the same time as the Irish festivals of Lughnasa.

So, it would seem, the 'lost' deities of the pagan Celtic world are not really lost at all, only lurking, often in a different guise, awaiting rediscovery and recognition in the future.

Magic birds and enchanted animals

The Celts believed that the gods and goddesses they worshipped took on not only the shapes and forms of animals and birds, but also their special qualities and characteristics. Certain animals were especially associated with the gods and these were treated with particular respect, as if they were the gods themselves.

For the men, the boar undoubtedly took pride of place and its courage when held at bay by the hunters was taken as an example of how warriors should behave in battle. Its meat, too, was a special favourite in feasting halls and both in this world and in the Otherworld lives were lost over the *curadmir*, the choicest portion of meat which was presented to the finest hero in the community. Divine boars and sacred sows appear in many of the old legends, often bringing great blessings with them. Boar-hunting was a favourite occupation of the Celtic aristocracy and is often shown in Celtic art. One statue of a god, from Euffigneix, Haute-Marne, France, has a huge boar emblazoned on his body. Some of the swine from the Otherworld had special magic powers: they could be killed and eaten one night, but appear again as a live pig the next day.

Stags were also important animals and were especially associated with the god known as Cernunnos 'the horned one', who is shown as a human figure wearing a pair of mighty antlers. They, too, were hunted for food and in the stories they were often used to entice their hunters into the Otherworld realms. Sometimes humans or even gods were transformed into deer. The son of the mighty Fionn was born from a goddess who had been changed into one by a druid's curse. She was already carrying Fionn's child and it was said that it would only be human if she did not lick its tiny body when it was born. By the time her son was born, however, her animal instincts were too strong and she could not keep herself from licking its forehead. Although the child grew up as a human being, he always had a tuft of animal hair growing on his forehead and from this he took his name, Oisin (Ossian), or 'Little deer'.

Birds were very important to the Celts who showed both in their art and in their legends that they had a deep and sympathetic knowledge of the different species. Some were considered birds of omen, the raven being especially associated with war and trouble.

Cranes were usually said to be goddesses who had been transformed and it was ill luck for a warrior to meet one as he went into battle. Cockerels, cranes and geese were tabu and could not be eaten except during religious rituals and there are stories of evil hawks and other dangerous birds of prey. Some birds, however, had the power to heal sorrow and bring joy with their songs. Swans were always thought to be birds of good omen, symbols of love and purity. In the Hebrides to this day, people will never kill a swan, and if anyone does so they are severely criticized by the whole community.

Humans or gods were frequently transformed into swans, often by a jealous rival; a swan with a chain of gold around its neck was sure to be a person in disguise and faithful lovers in their swan form were often linked together by fine chains of gold. The story of Midir and Etain shows the sacred swan as a messenger of love, a theme which occurs time and again in Celtic mythology and folklore.

The god Midir, lord of the *sidh* mound of Bri Leith, a hill in County Longford in Ireland, once fell in love with a beautiful immortal girl named Etain. After an ardent courtship he married her and brought her to his home in the *sidh*. However, he already had a wife named Fuamnach and she was bitterly jealous of her beautiful, young rival. One day she could bear it no longer and she struck Etain with her magic wand, transforming her into a pool of water. As she stood gloating over her triumph, the pool began to change into a serpent which hissed at her sadly before in turn changing into a superb, purple-winged dragon-fly. The dragon-fly fluttered off, its fine wings shimmering in the sunlight, and Fuamnach returned to Midir, happy to be his only wife once more.

Midir had no choice but to accept the situation for he could not undo the spell and he did not wish to punish Fuamnach whom he still loved. As for the dragon-fly, it never left Midir's side and went with him everywhere. Midir knew that it was his beloved Etain and took care that no harm should come to it.

Fuamnach was angry that she had not finally managed to destroy her rival and one day, when Midir and his dragon-fly were sitting together outside, she called up a magic gust of wind which blew the dragon-fly far up into the air and carried it away, over the hills and forests to the sea shore. The magic wind dropped the dragon-fly on the lonely shore and there for seven long years it lived in misery and discomfort, its delicate wings battered and soaked by the cold salt spray.

One day, when seven years had passed, Angus, the god of love happened to walk along the shore and, catching sight of the dragon-fly's bright wings glinting among the rocks, he picked it gently up and carried it home with him. He made a crystal cage for it, filled it with flowers and herbs and from then on took it everywhere with him.

Soon everyone was talking about Angus's marvellous dragon-fly and the story reached Midir and Fuamnach in Bri Leith. However, before Midir could find out more, Fuamnach managed to steal the cage from Angus. She opened the door to free the dragon-fly, then as it fluttered to freedom, called up another magic wind which drove it away once more. Helplessly it was tossed all over Ireland until eventually it was blown onto the roof of a great stronghold in Ulster and fell through the smoke-hole into the feasting hall, straight into the cup from which the woman of the house, Etar, was drinking. The woman swallowed it without noticing and nine months later gave birth to a baby daughter whom she named Etain.

Although Etain had the same name as before, she had no memory of her previous life nor of her unhappy years as a dragon-fly and she grew up into a beautiful young woman.

Now at that time Eochaid Airem was the high king of Ireland and all the other monarchs obeyed him. At the end of his first year of kingship he commanded that a splendid feast should be held at Tara to celebrate the anniversary. In spite of his powerful position, no one would come to the feast for he was not married and this was considered to be a serious fault in a king. So Eochaid sent messengers throughout the whole of Ireland to find a suitable bride. They visited the household of

every chieftain in Ireland and as soon as they saw Etain they knew that she was the most fitting. At once Eochaid hurried to visit her and claim her as his bride.

He found her sitting on the green lawn at Bri Leith, beside a spring of bright, bubbling water. She was loosening her hair to wash it, unfastening it from the golden balls which held it and combing it with a shimmering silver comb inlaid with gold. On the grass beside her was a washing bowl, also made of silver, inlaid with gems and decorated with four golden birds. Her fair, white arms were bare though a rich purple cloak hung from her shoulders and Eochaid could see that she wore a robe with edgings of silver and a green silk tunic embroidered with gold and fastened with pins of shining silver and gleaming gold.

Eochaid fell in love with Etain as soon as he saw her and he stood amazed by her beauty. Her cheeks were like wild foxgloves, her eyes as blue as the hyacinth and her skin, as luminous as new-fallen snow, made her lips seem even more brilliantly red. Everything about her was perfect—from her long, tapering fingers to her slender ankles and neat, narrow feet. Eochaid and his companions were sure that she must belong to the Otherworld people of the *sidh* mound but when he asked for her hand she told him she was the daughter of Etar and that she had been in love with him since childhood. They were married at once and everyone rejoiced at the king's suitable choice.

Before long the Otherworld people of Bri Leith heard about Etain's outstanding beauty and Midir realized that this must be the same girl who had been his wife long years ago. Disguising himself as a young man he hurried to her at Tara. He told Etain who she really was, and how she had been his wife.

'Why did you leave me, then?' asked Etain, who still remembered nothing of her past life. 'The evil magic of Fuamnach took you from me,' he replied. 'Come back with me to your home in the Otherworld.'

Etain refused his pleading scornfully. 'I will not give up the high king of Ireland for you,' she said. 'Why should I believe you when I do not even remember you?'

Midir left, defeated, but a short time later he returned to Tara, this time in his true form as a splendid young warrior. He introduced himself to Eochaid and explained that he had come to play a game of chess with him. Eochaid was said to be the best player in the country and before they began he asked what stakes they should play for.

'Let the loser pay whatever is asked of him,' Midir said.

'I agree,' Eochaid replied, confident that he would be the winner, and the game began.

They played several games and each time Midir allowed Eochaid to win and gave him everything he asked for as a reward. In the last game, however, Midir easily defeated the over-confident king.

'What do you want?' asked Eochaid.

'To take Etain in my arms and kiss her,' replied Midir.

Eochaid was silent for a moment but he could not break his word so finally he said, 'Come here a month from today and you shall have what you want.'

Midir left promising to return in a month's time. Immediately Eochaid consulted the druids to see what could be done. On their advice he summoned all the warriors of Ireland to guard Tara on the day Midir was expected. For, the druids said, if Midir could not come to Etain on the day he had specified, Eochaid's promise would no longer be binding on him.

The day came and the gates of Tara were firmly barred. Eochaid and Etain stood in the innermost room of the palace, surrounded by a circle of warriors, certain that no harm could come to them.

Suddenly, from out of the air, Midir was standing there inside the circle of bristling spears and for the first time Etain saw him as he really was, without any disguise. If he had seemed fair before, he was divinely beautiful now and when he said, 'Eochaid promised I could take you in my arms,' she made no resistance.

With his first kiss, Etain's memory returned: she remembered how much she had loved Midir and knew that she loved him still.

'Take me with you,' she said.

Before Eochaid and his warriors could move to prevent it, Midir had taken his weapons in one hand, seized Etain with the other and carried her off with him through the smoke-hole.

The king and his men ran outside to see if they could catch them but there was no sign of either the warrior or the beautiful Etain. All they could see were two swans, linked together by chains of gold about their necks. The two circled slowly around Tara then flew off towards the *sidh* at Bri Leith, their great wings beating in harmony, their golden chains shining in the sun.

And so Midir won back his wife Etain from the high king of Ireland and carried her home to live contentedly with him in the Otherworld.

The Land of Promise

This story about King Cormac of Ireland is one of a group of legends about the kings of early Ireland where historical fact is mingled with stories remembered from the early days of the Celts. In it, the human king is spirited away to the Otherworld, where magic animals and birds seem almost a part of everyday life.

Early one May morning, King Cormac was alone in Tara, the chief fortress of the high kings of Ireland. There he saw a distinguished, grey-haired warrior coming towards him, wearing a purple fringed cloak with threads of gold and with shoes made of white bronze on his feet. In his hand he carried a silver branch which bore three golden apples and made magic music. So sweet was the sound it made that everyone who heard it fall into a deep, peaceful sleep, even women suffering in childbed or warriors lying awake with the pain of their wounds.

'Where have you come from?' asked the king.

'From a land where there is truth alone and no envy,' replied the stranger. 'Where there is no age nor decay, no gloom, no sorrow and no pride.'

'We are not like that,' said the king, 'but it would be an excellent thing if my kingdom and yours were to be allied. Shall we make a pact of friendship?'

'I should like that,' replied the stranger.

'May I have the branch to seal our pact?' asked the king.

'You may have it as long as you grant me three requests,' replied the stranger.

'They are granted,' said the king and the stranger gave him the branch and went on his way.

'I will return,' he said.

Cormac returned to his palace and showed the magic branch to his people. When he shook it over them they heard the sweet, soft music and the whole court fell deeply asleep for a

night and a day. Pleased with his new power, Cormac forgot his promise to the stranger and life continued as usual.

In due course the stranger came to the palace and made the first of his requests.
'Give me your daughter, Ailbe,' he said.

The women began to wail but Cormac was a man of his word; he gave his daughter to the calm stranger and shook the branch over the weeping women so that they were soothed and fell asleep, forgetful of their loss.

Some time later the warrior came a second time and this time he asked for Cormac's son Cairbre. Again, Cormac kept his word and again there was great weeping in the court until he shook the magic branch and all became peaceful.

The third time the stranger returned he asked for Cormac's own wife, the queen of Ireland herself, and this time Cormac was tested beyond endurance. He allowed the stranger to leave with the queen but instead of waving the branch over his court to soothe them, he called them to arms and urged them to follow him in pursuit.

In the middle of a plain a druidic mist came down, swirling thickly around them and separating the king from his men. Then the mist in front of him cleared and he saw a fortress on the plain, surrounded by a wall of bronze. Inside the fortress was a house made of white silver, thatched with thousands of white feathers. Around the house were teams of Otherworld horsemen who were busy rethatching the roof, their arms full of the wings of white birds. Beside them a man was kindling a fire with a great oak tree.

Looking around, Cormac saw a second fortress, again containing a palace thatched with white feathers, this time with beams of bronze and wattles of silver. Inside its stockade was a bright fountain from which flowed five clear streams. Nine sacred hazel trees grew over the fountain and their purple-shelled nuts fell into the water to feed the five salmon who lived there. The noise of the falling streams and the fountain made magic, melodious music and all around were Otherworld people, drinking from the five clear streams.

As if in a dream, Cormac entered the great hall of this palace. There he found a handsome young warrior and a beautiful girl with a head-dress of gold to match her golden hair. Unseen hands guided him to a seat, washed his feet and bathed him in a pool of water heated by glowing stones. When Cormac began to feel hungry, he saw a man coming into the hall carrying an axe and a log and followed by a pig. 'It is time to eat,' said the young warrior and immediately the man with the axe killed the pig, kindled a fire from the log and began to roast the carcass on a spit.
'Now turn the pig so that it is cooked evenly,' said the warrior.
'It is impossible to turn the spit unless a true story is told,' said the man, 'and I will need to hear a true story for each quarter of the meat.'
'Then tell the first one yourself,' said the young warrior.
'One day,' began the man, 'when I was walking around my land, I found someone else's cattle grazing there. I took them to the cattle pound and their owner came along and said he would reward me if I set them free. I did so and in return he gave me a pig, an axe and a log. He said that every night the axe would split the log and kill the pig; and every day the log would be whole and the pig would be alive again. And so it was for this is the very same log and this the very same pig you see before you today.'
'Well,' said the young warrior, 'that is certainly a true story. Turn the pig and I'll tell you the next one myself. Once it was ploughing time but when we came to plough the field, we found it was already not only ploughed but harrowed and sown with wheat as well. When reaping time came, we set out with our knives only to find the wheat was cut and stacked in the field. The next day we went to bring it in but there it was already, safe and dry under the thatched rick.
'And although we have eaten it every day since then, the pile of grain never grows less and never grows old.'

The man nodded and turned the pig on the spit. A second quarter was cooked.
'Now it is my turn,' said the young woman. 'I have no more than seven cows and seven sheep

said he would not eat until his followers were reunited with him. Then the man with the axe sang a soft, sweet song and Cormac fell into a deep sleep. When he awoke he found that not only were his men around him but that his daughter, his son and his wife were with them, too.

The young warrior and the beautiful girl urged them all to eat and drink and there was great feasting and merriment in the hall. When they had eaten, the young warrior stood up and an unseen servant placed a beautifully decorated golden cup in his hand.

'There are two strange things about this cup,' said the warrior. 'If three falsehoods are uttered it will break into three pieces. But if three truths are told, it will be whole again.' To demonstrate its powers, the warrior made two false statements and then said that Cormac's wife had a new husband; sure enough, the marvellous cup broke into three pieces.

'I had better tell you the truth,' said the warrior, 'so that it may become whole again. I tell you Cormac that, until today, your wife has not set eyes on a man since she was taken from Tara; neither has your daughter; and your son has not set eyes on a woman until he came to this hall.'

Immediately the three pieces of gold joined together and the cup was whole and perfect again.

'Now take your family,' said the warrior, 'and take the cup so that you can tell truth from falsehood; and keep the magic branch that I gave you to give you music and sweet sleep. For I am Manannan mac Lir, the stranger you met in the sanctuary at Tara, and king of the Land of Promise. I brought you here so that you could see this country with which you are allied, where there is truth and no envy, no age nor decay, no gloom or sorrow and no pride. When you die the cup and the branch will be taken from you, but now enjoy them while you live.'

These were the last words that Cormac heard in the Land of Promise for he fell fast asleep as Manannan spoke and when he awoke, he found himself back on the green at Tara with his wife and his son and his daughter, his golden cup

but the milk from the seven cows is enough to satisfy all the people of the Land of Promise and they make all the clothing they need from the wool of the seven sheep. And that is my true story.'

Again the man nodded. A third quarter of the pig was cooked and they said to Cormac, 'Now it is your turn to tell a story.'

Cormac told how his daughter and his son and his wife had been taken from him and how he had set out in search of them. As he spoke he wept and they knew that what he said was true.

The pig was ready to be eaten but Cormac

and his magic branch beside him.

Long after King Cormac had died, when the world of the Celts had been transformed by the coming of Christianity, another visitor found his way to the magical Land of Promise. This was Saint Brendan of Clonfert in County Galway, whose voyage in a skin boat to a land across the ocean has been claimed as the first visit by a European to America.

The tale was written down around the ninth century AD but on the perilous journey the adventurers found themselves in realms more familiar to the druids than to Christian monks, with monsters and magic animals from the Celtic past.

Saint Brendan was head of some 3000 monks at Clonfert in western Ireland and one evening a monk named Father Barinthus came to see him. He had been on a visit to a hermit who now lived on an island called the Island of Delights. While he was there, the hermit had invited Barinthus to sail with him westwards to an island known as the 'Island of Promise of the Saints'. They set out in their small ox-hide boat and soon ran into a patch of dense fog. As they rowed out to the other side of it, they found themselves near a large island full of luscious fruit trees and flowers. They stayed there for fifteen days, exploring the beauties of the place

but one day they came to a river which flowed right across from east to west. A stranger appeared on the bank, forbidding them to cross to the other half of the island and telling them to go home. He escorted them back to the shore and then vanished as suddenly as he had appeared. No sooner had they pushed off from land than the dense fog surrounded them once more. As soon as it cleared, they found themselves within sight of Ireland.

Brendan was fascinated by the story and at once chose fourteen of his monks to go with him to find this wonderful island in the far west. First they fasted for forty days, then built a boat with a wooden frame, stretched tanned ox-hides over it, put a mast and sail on board and loaded it with supplies to last them for forty days.

After fifteen days of sailing towards the west they were completely lost and when they came to a rocky island they decided to land. There was no sign of human life but a solitary dog came to them and led them to a house where a meal was laid ready. They stayed for three days and though they saw no-one, their meals were always set out for them on the table. It was only when they were climbing back into their boat that a young man came up to them, offering them loaves of bread and fresh water.

Next they came to the Island of Sheep where there were sheep as big as oxen. Here another young man brought them food. He told them about the journey that lay ahead and offered to travel with them as their guide and protector on their journey through the Otherworld.

The next island was stony and the monks hauled up their boat, lit a fire, and began to cook some mutton they had brought from the Island of Sheep. As it began to boil the whole island started to move and to shake violently and they fled back to their boat in terror. They reached it just in time for the island was really a gigantic sea-monster and it dived beneath the waves with their fire still blazing on it.

Then they reached the Paradise of Birds where they found a great tree with birds clinging to it like great white buds. One of the birds flew down and told Brendan that the birds were in fact the souls of men and that it would take him seven years to reach the Land of Promise. The birds sang and chanted with them at their services but soon the Otherworld youth appeared and they set off once more.

For seven long years they sailed across the sea, driven from island to island by the wind, terrified by fire-breathing monsters and often in fear of their lives. Whenever they landed, the Otherworld youth was waiting for them to give them food and clothing.

At long last he led them to the 'Island of Promise of the Saints' and there they saw all the marvellous things the holy men had described. On the bank of the river which ran from east to west they, too, met a young man who told them to return home, for Brendan, he said, was soon to die.

As they set sail, a magical mist engulfed the little boat once more and before they knew it, they were within sight of home: the journey that had taken seven long years was over in a moment.

A few years ago a man named Tim Severin built an ox-hide curragh and proved that a boat like the one Saint Brendan used could actually have made the dangerous voyage to America. But whether the Land of Promise lay across the ocean or in the mysterious Otherworld you must decide for yourself.

Celtic cats

Horses, dogs, magical sheep, wolves, serpents and animals of all kinds play important parts in Celtic mythology. The Celts also feared and respected cats although they never held them in any affection as domestic pets. To them, the cat symbolized dark supernatural powers, tyranny and death, and carvings of cats often appear on grave stones in parts of the Celtic world.

Cats have amazing psychic powers and powers of survival—their nine lives are a true assessment of their independence and toughness. In Celtic times fierce wild cats were common in Europe and some of the Celts would have seen lions and larger cats on their travels. The yowling of tom cats on the prowl on bright moonlit nights is quite blood-curdling, and to a people as superstitious as the Celts all these factors must have made a deep impression. Cats are still important in folklore, where they are often sinister animals, linked closely to the world of the supernatural.

Cath Palug was a monster cat, and the stories told about him and other supernatural cats are probably reminders of a sinister god who appeared in the form of a cat and was feared and worshipped with rituals and sacrifices. Stories were told about him in many parts of Europe, especially in France, where he is called Le Capalu and appears in medieval tales about King Arthur. This story of his birth comes from Wales.

There was once a swineherd named Coll who was charged with guarding a magical sow. She roamed about the countryside with Coll following after, trying to control her. While she was expecting her litter she was especially difficult to guard and she raced from one part of the land to another. First she ran to north Cornwall where she dived into the sea, dragging Coll with her because he never let go of her bristles. She swam with him across the sea to Gwent in south-east Wales and there she gave birth not to a litter of piglets but to a single grain of wheat and a bee. Ever afterwards, the place where she landed was known for the fine quality of its wheat and honey. Next the sow ran to Pembroke, south-west Wales, and there

she lay down again to have her litter. This time she gave birth to a single grain of barley and a bee. On she went towards the north, producing on the way first a wolf-cub and then an eaglet. At last she reached the north coast and there on the rocky shore opposite the island of Anglesey, she gave birth to a kitten.

As soon as he saw it, Coll knew that this was no ordinary kitten. It was as large as a horse, with great yellow eyes, sharply pointed teeth and fierce, menacing claws.
'Nothing but evil will come from you,' said Coll to himself and, seizing the monster cat with both hands, he strode to the edge of the rock and flung it as far as he could into the sea.

The fall alone would have been enough for most cats but not for this one. No sooner did it hit the waves than it struck out strongly for the opposite shore, forcing its way through the sea like a powerful sailing boat. The sons of Palug found it roaming the shore of Anglesey in search of food and they took it in and reared it so that forever after it was known as Cath Palug, or Palug's cat.

But Coll had been right when he said that nothing but evil would come from it; instead of being grateful for the help of the sons of Palug, the cat did so much harm to their land and people that it became known as one of the three great oppressions of Anglesey.

A long, long time after this strange birth, Saint Brendan and his monks met a very similar monster cat as they voyaged in search of the Land of Promise. One day they ran into a terrible storm. Peering out through the clouds of spray they saw a rocky island in the distance and steered gratefully towards it. A giant wave carried their boat safely ashore and they jumped out to pull it clear of the pounding waves. Suddenly, above the roar of the wind, they heard a voice calling out to them.
'Go back,' it said. 'Go back to the sea. You are in great danger here.'

An old, ragged man was clambering down the cliffs towards them, waving his arms and shouting.
'What danger can be worse than this storm?' asked Saint Brendan. 'Our boat is small and will never ride these waves.'

'The danger here is greater still,' said the old man. 'A monster cat lives on this island and he will devour you all. He came with my companions and me to settle here, as playful and charming a kitten as ever you saw. But as soon as he had explored the place, he began to ignore the food we put out for him. Instead he ate the strange fish that were washed up on the shore and from then on his nature changed. He grew huge and fierce, he spat at us if we tried to come near him and attacked anything, man or beast, that crossed his path. By now he has grown so large that no-one is safe. I myself have only survived through great vigilance.'

As he spoke, a blood-curdling yowl echoed from the cliffs, a cry louder even than the wind, full of power and menace. Saint Brendan and his monks did not wait to see what the monster looked like but sprang back into the boat and pushed off as quickly as they could.

The tide carried them swiftly away from the shore and soon they looked back to see what was happening to the old man. They saw an animal as large as a small pony bounding across the sand and leaping into the water. To their horror, it began to swim towards them, moving through the waves with ease. The monks could see its great paws paddling through the water and its eyes, like great circles of yellow glass, shining through the storm.
'It is a devil,' cried one of the monks.
'Let us pray for help,' said Saint Brendan, 'for we cannot outrun this monster.'

They knelt down in the rolling boat and prayed as hard as they had ever prayed before. When they peered cautiously over the side, they were just in time to see a second cat, as monstrous as the first, rising from the depths of the sea. As the first cat reached out its paw to clamber on board, the second bit down on its tail and dragged it away.

The cats whirled and floundered in the water, biting and scratching and hissing like two snakes. Then suddenly it was quiet again. In their frenzy, the cats had pulled each other down under the waves. As they vanished, the rain stopped; the wind died down, the sea grew calm again and Saint Brendan and his monks sailed safely on in their small boat.

The giants of Morvah

Western Cornwall has always been famous for its giants, especially around Morvah, which lies on the north-western slopes of the wind and weather-swept promontory of Land's End. The Cornish language was spoken here until the end of the eighteenth century and the people were so isolated from the rest of the country that they kept customs and beliefs long after they had become mere folk-memories elsewhere. In the nineteenth century two great Cornish folklore collectors, Robert Hunt and William Bottrell, wrote down many of these old beliefs and legends.

The tales are long and complex—it is said that one of the Morvah stories took three nights to tell. The one told here is about a giant named Tom and his skilful visitor Jack. Some think that the giants were the ancient Celtic gods in a new disguise; and that Jack the skilful stranger is none other than the all-skilled god Lugh.

One midsummer eve Tom was driving home to Morvah from St Ives when he found the road blocked by rocks which had been piled on top of each other to make a dry stone wall. Unable to go round them and too tired to move them one by one, he decided to take a short cut across some land belonging to the giant who lived in a castle nearby. As he drew near the castle, the giant ran out. 'What are you doing on my land?' he bellowed.
'You have blocked the road with your hedges,' replied Tom calmly. 'You have no right to do that; so I am taking my own way home.'

Furiously, the giant seized a young elm tree, pulled it up by the roots and brandished it threateningly. 'Get off my land,' he roared.

Calmly, Tom overturned his wagon, removed the wheel and axle and stood to face the giant. What a fight began then as the two huge figures strode across the hills and moorlands, wielding their mighty weapons and making the ground shake with their blows. At last Tom struck the giant on the neck and he fell down dead.

Half dead himself with exhaustion, Tom looked down from the hill. Far below he could see the people dancing around the festive fires but he knew that he must bury the giant and take possession of his land. First of all, however, he went to visit a woman named Joan, whom he had been courting for many years. She bathed his wounds and agreed to go with him to the giant's castle.

It was dawn when they arrived and the guard dogs barked fiercely at them. When Tom called out their names, however, they allowed the pair to enter the caves beside the castle. These were full to the brim with treasures, for the giant had been a great hoarder of gold and precious jewels. Realizing that they were now rich, Joan and Tom buried the giant and raised a cairn above him. All the land they could see for miles about them, and all the cattle grazing on the hills now belonged to them and there they lived in peace and happiness. When he was not working his land, Tom was busy strengthening his own stone hedges to keep curious people away from his treasure.

One morning when they had been living like this for many years, Tom heard someone hammering on the gate.

'Who is that?' he bellowed. 'I don't care who you are, you're not getting in.'

But before he had finished speaking, the gate had been smashed and in walked a travelling tinker with his tool bag on his back. He was as large as Tom himself and in one hand he brandished a hammer.

'Where do you think you are going?' Tom demanded.

'I'm taking the old road to St Ives in spite of your gates and hedges,' the stranger replied. 'The people all around are complaining about them. I suppose a fine, sturdy fellow like you must be the giant's son. Would you like a friendly fight?'

'Gladly,' Tom replied, 'and you can choose the weapons. We can wrestle or box or sling stones—the choice is yours.'

'Right,' said the tinker whose name was Jack. 'I'll use my blackthorn staff.'

Tom seized a broken axle beam and they began to fight, but Jack took hold of his staff in the middle and spun it round Tom's head so quickly that it looked like a spinning wheel. Tom stood watching it dizzily until with one deft movement Jack stopped it in mid-air and with a single blow sent Tom's own weapon flying over the fence.

'Now, dear boy, you'd really better give in. This game requires intelligence as much as strength,' said the tinker. Tom was ashamed but the tinker seemed good natured enough and when he offered to teach Tom some tricks with his staff, the two soon became good friends.

When they had eaten a meal together, Tom and Jack went hunting. Tom only had a sling but that did not worry clever Jack. In no time he had cut an elm sapling and made it into a bow, strung with a cord from his work-bag which seemed to contain everything you could ever need. Then he notched and feathered a good set of arrows and in the time Tom took to bring down one animal with his sling, Jack had killed ten. Joan was delighted with all the venison, the hares and rabbits they brought back from the hills.

While Joan's eldest daughter, Genevra, helped her mother with the supper, Tom took Jack all round his treasure-caves but Jack was more impressed by any bits and pieces that would help him with his work than with all the jewels and the plates of silver and gold. When they were called to supper, the tinker searched in his bag, produced a string of pearls, placed it on Genevra's head and took his place at the table beside her.

Jack was invited to stay the night and the next, and the next. In fact he liked it so much there that he stayed forever and eventually married Tom's daughter Genevra. The marriage took place on the first Sunday of August and every year after that, when the tinker's wedding day came round, all their relations came from far and near to celebrate the anniversary. They stayed a week or more hunting and feasting and playing the ancient games for as long as the daylight lasted. Jack taught the others skills they never knew existed and together they had many happy adventures.

In a few years time there were so many friends and relations coming to Morvah on the first Sunday in August that the event began to seem more like a fair than a wedding anniversary; and that is the origin of the great Morvah Fair which is still held today.

The giants have all disappeared from Cornwall now but some people still imagine them striding over the land, their great bodies outlined against the sky as they fight their mighty battles in the clouds.

Gods of the landscape

Most of what we know about ancient Celtic mythology comes from the comments of contemporary Greek and Roman writers, from archaeological remains and from folklore handed down from generation to generation. But there is another mysterious source of information: figures cut into the chalk of southern England and etched upon the harder rocks elsewhere. The most famous are the Cerne Abbas Giant in Dorset, the Long Man of Wilmington and the White Horse of Uffington.

The Cerne Abbas Giant was probably first carved into the chalk hills by a tribe of Celts known as the Durotriges who lived in this region two thousand years ago. This figure of a naked man shaking a club must surely have been an image of one of their gods, probably one rather like Cernunnos the horned god or Sucellos the Good Striker. The Giant measures 61 metres (200 feet) from the soles of his feet to the top of the club which he brandishes aggressively above his head. The people remembered him as a bringer of fertility long after the coming of Christianity. On the slope below his massive figure is a well and by its side grows an old grey hazel tree. On the eve of their marriage, young couples used to visit the giant and on the way down the hill, the lad would carry his girl across the stream, then collect a hazel twig to ensure the blessing of their marriage.

It may be that several other figures were once cut into chalk hills both in Britain and elsewhere but have since been destroyed by time, cultivation or for religious reasons. The Long Man of Wilmington, however, has survived on the downs of East Sussex. This elongated, elegant figure measures some 69 metres (226 feet) in height and may date from no later than the seventh century AD. It is half as tall again as the Statue of Liberty and is the second largest representation of the human form in history, since only the Inca Giant of Atacama exceeds it.

This great figure carries a staff or spear in each hand and one of the stories told about him is that he was a living giant who slipped on the steep slope and broke his neck in his fall. When he died, the people laid him out on the hillside and cut his shape in the turf over the chalk so that future generations would know about him. In mediaeval times it was believed that he had been killed by devout pilgrims but this story may have been made up because the church disapproved of such an obviously pagan figure in the middle of the countryside. Another legend told that it was the giant's duty to make sure that there would be a large number of healthy lambs and a good harvest each year. In one year, though, the lambing was poor and the crops failed, so the giant was killed by a shepherd who considered that he was no longer of any use to the community.

A very different hill figure is the White Horse at Uffington. Here, bounding and bouncing across the green turf just beside a hillfort, is the symbol of the powerful Celtic horse goddess Epona. The White Horse, like the other hillside figures, was regularly cleared of grass to keep its shape clean and bright, visible for miles around. The task was turned into a festival, with horse and donkey racing, wrestling and the rolling of cheeses down the hillside. It is considered lucky to make a wish while standing in the Horse's eye. Another white horse, at Westbury in Wiltshire, was recut in the eighteenth century. It was turned into a fat, pompous animal but its original outline may once have closely resembled Epona's elegance.

Figures of giants and horses created by cutting turf from the underlying chalk are spectacular when seen from some distance away. Heads carved into harder rock are less spectacular but equally important. A fine example is a group of eight heads outlined on a massive boulder crowning a moorland area just seven miles north of Glasgow city centre. At Entremont, Bouches-du-Rhône, France a splendid stone slab is covered with twelve incised faces piled on top of each other.

Many people assume that the ancient groups of standing stones at Stonehenge in England and Carnac, France were also erected by the historical Celts but this is not the case.

Stonehenge is a circle of massive standing stones; other blocks form cross-pieces and the whole site is enclosed by a circular bank. The stark, grey purposeful pillars dominate the bleak moorland around it but although there are many theories about its origins, there has never

been a universally accepted explanation of its purpose. A twelfth century historian, Geoffrey of Monmouth, wrote that Stonehenge had been magically transported from Ireland by Merlin the magician and placed on Salisbury Plain as a monument to a group of dead British chieftains. In fact, Stonehenge was built in stages from about 2600 BC onwards, some two thousand years before the rise of the Celts, though they may well have used it for their religious ceremonies as do modern 'druids' on mid-summer's day. A Roman writer described a magnificent circular temple of Apollo in the centre of Britain where the citizens chanted and played on their harps in honour of the sun: perhaps he was referring to Stonehenge.

The famous and impressive Lines of Carnac in Brittany are also much earlier than the Celts. They consist of several thousand standing stones that were set up over four thousand years ago and arranged in lines that stretch out over the countryside for vast distances. Again, their original purpose is a mystery, and there are many folk-tales about them.

One explanation of their origin is that they were columns of hostile, pagan soldiers who were turned into stone before they could attack and kill Saint Cornély, the patron saint of

Carnac. On Christmas Eve once in a hundred years, the stones slowly make their way to the nearest river to drink, leaving hoardes of gold unguarded in their holes. Yet although the stones go slowly to the river, they return extremely swiftly and any plunderer will be crushed to death unless he or she carries a branch of mistletoe surrounded by a five-leaved clover. Even then, the gold will crumble into dust before sunrise unless a Christian soul is given in exchange for it.

The naming of places

It is in Ireland that the ancient deities can be traced most clearly in the names of the country's landmarks. 'The Story of the Important Places', known in Ireland as the *Dindshenchas*, is a collection of legends explaining how and why certain places received their names. Hidden among the logical explanations lies a wealth of information about pagan Celtic Ireland. The collection is vast, and was finally written down by Irish monks in the twelfth century AD. This story tells how Inber-n-Aillbine was given its name.

Ruad was a prince of Ireland and one of the best and bravest men in the kingdom. He had many friends and no enemies, and was welcome wherever he went. One day he decided to visit his foster-brother, the son of the king of Norway, and he set sail from Ireland with a fleet of three ships. The weather was fine and the wind was fresh, and very soon the little fleet was halfway across the sea. Suddenly all three ships jerked to a halt as if they had run into an invisible wall. The sailors could not make the ships move in any direction, however hard they tried. Indeed, it felt as if they were somehow anchored to the seabed so firmly fixed were they.

Ruad ordered his ships' captains to wait for him for as long as possible and then dived over the side of his ship to find out what was holding them fast. As he swam beneath the boat he was amazed to see nine of the most beautiful women in the world floating beneath the waves. Each maiden had eyes that were one of the many colours of the sea: one had cool grey eyes, another sea-green and yet another of the deepest blue that Ruad had ever seen. Three of them were under each ship and were holding on to the keels to prevent them from moving. When they saw Ruad, the women swam

123

towards him, clasped him firmly in their strong arms and carried him downwards to their Otherworld home.

Ruad stayed with them for nine days but although they gave him everything he could wish for, he soon began to feel homesick and longed to escape from the strange land beneath the sea. Gradually he sank into a deep melancholy. The women noticed his distress and asked him what was wrong.
'I should like to visit my foster-brother,' Ruad sighed. 'We have not met since boyhood, and now I shall never see him again.'
'If you leave us, you will never come back to us,' one of the women said. 'It is better that you remain here.'
'If you let me go, I promise that I shall return to you,' Ruad said. 'If you love me, you should also trust me when I say that I will not desert you.'

Reluctantly the women agreed, carried him safely back to his ship, and sent him on his way to his foster-brother's stronghold. Ruad was warmly welcomed by the Norwegian prince and stayed with him for seven years, but eventually he had to return to his own country. Although he set out in his ships once more, Ruad did not keep his promise of returning to the realm of the strange women, but urged his men to sail as fast as they could for Ireland.

Now while Ruad had lived in the undersea kingdom he had slept with one of the women and she had given birth to a son, who was now nearly seven years old. When the women realized that Ruad was breaking his promise to return, they seized the child and set out after him in a bronze boat, singing an unearthly song as they went. Inexorably, they gained on Ruad's ship and he was about to give up in despair when he saw the faint outline of the Irish coast on the horizon. He urged his men to row faster but still the bronze boat came closer and closer. Just before it caught up with them, however, they landed in Ireland and Ruad leaped ashore ahead of them.

Then the mother of the little boy—Ruad's only son—did a terrible thing: she killed the child and hurled his severed head on to the land after his father.

'It is a dreadful deed! It is a dreadful crime!' the watchers cried in horror and for this reason the place where it all happened was called for ever afterwards 'The Bay of the Dreadful Shout' or in Irish Inber-n-Aillbine.

As for the nine strange women, they sailed away in their bronze boat and were never heard of again; but for the rest his life Ruad never sailed on the water again.

The golden idol

One grim legend told to explain how Mag Slecht, 'The Plain of Prostration', got its name, seems to describe an ancient circle of standing stones and a fearful ritual of human sacrifice that took place there. A golden idol, it was said, used to stand on Mag Slecht, surrounded by eleven lesser idols made of stone. The golden idol was known as Crom Dubh and the people worshipped it and paid it a hard tribute to protect themselves from its evil influence. It demanded human sacrifice and the people were forced to offer it their first-born children. In return for this, they asked for rich yields of milk and corn and for the harvest to be free of blight and disease.

In the old days the people bowed down and prostrated themselves before the idol, beating their palms and bruising their bodies in the violence of their worship: from this the plain received its name. The god Lugh fought against Crom Dubh for possession of the harvest but it was not until the coming of Saint Patrick that its power was finally overthrown.

When Patrick came to Mag Slecht on his travels through Ireland, he went up to the idol to lay his cross on its head and drive the demon away. As he did so, the great idol bowed to the west, turning to its right side; and at the same time the earth swallowed up the eleven stone idols around it so that only their heads remained above the ground. Then Patrick took a mighty sledge-hammer and split the golden god from head to foot, sending its demon fleeing helplessly to the Otherworld. And so the power of Crom Dubh was broken for ever.

The two birds

There is a place on the River Shannon in Ireland with the curious name Snamh da en, or 'The swimming of the two birds'. This is how it took its name.

There was once a man named Nar who lived in the province of Connacht with his wife Estiu, a woman warrior. Now Estiu was a very beautiful woman and it happened that a man named Buide fell in love with her and decided to try to take her from her husband. Buide had a foster-brother who went with him everywhere and the two men came to Nar's house to woo Estiu in the form of birds.

The birds perched on the branches of a tree beside the house and sang so sweetly that all the people came out to listen and were lulled into a deep sleep. Estiu, however, was too intrigued to sleep and as soon as the others were safely unconscious, Buide regained his human form and took her aside to woo her.

The birds came several times and each time the same thing happened. Eventually Nar became suspicious and he consulted his druid to find out the true nature of these sweetly singing birds.

The druid cast his spells and he swiftly discovered the brothers' real identities. When he explained that they were men in the shape of birds, Nar became furiously jealous. The very next day he lay in wait and when he saw the two brothers arriving in the shape of swans he hid in the reeds beside the river to trap them. The two graceful birds landed on the water and swam slowly round, waiting for Estiu to come to meet them as she had promised. As they waited, Nar stealthily pulled out his sling and casting with rage and bitterness, he killed them both with a single stone.

Nar's jealousy, however, brought nothing but evil to his family. Estiu was so heart-broken at the death of the two brothers that she pined away and died and Nar, unable to face life without her, also died of grief.

But ever since, the name of the place on the River Shannon where the two magic birds swam has kept their memory alive.

The Isle of Man

In the middle of the Irish Sea, at almost equal distances from Ireland, Scotland, England and Wales, lies the beautiful Isle of Man, which takes its name from Manannan, son of Lir, the ancient Irish god of the sea. Manannan takes the shape of a normal man in most of the legends, but he was once described as having three legs on which he could travel at great speed, and these three legs are now the symbol of the Isle of Man.

Manannan was a great illusionist and loved to play tricks on people. Once a chieftain called Aodh Dubh O'Donnell was holding a feast for his people and boasting about the wealth of his house and the skills of his musicians. As they were all talking, a strange figure came walking across the hall. He wore striped clothes and his shoes seemed to be full of water, for it slopped out all over the floor. His cloak was pulled over his head but his ears poked through the tattered cloth and his sword was stuck naked into his belt. In his hand he carried three scorched, blackened spears of holly wood and on his back was a large bag.
'Where have you come from?' asked O'Donnell.
'From round and about,' said the stranger.
'How did you get in? The gate keeper has orders to tell me when a stranger is at the gate.'
'Don't blame him,' said the stranger. 'It was easy for me to get in and it will be easy for me to get out again.'

At that moment the musicians O'Donnell had boasted about began to play and indeed they played the sweetest music in all Ireland. But the stranger clapped his hands over his ears and called out, 'Wherever did you find those players? I would rather listen to the sound of a hundred hammers on iron than to the noise they are making.'

Without a word, he took a harp himself and the music he plucked from its strings would have lulled the most anxious heart, the most pain-wracked body into peaceful sleep.
'Since I first heard the music of the *sidh* mounds I have never heard music like yours,' O'Donnell said. 'You are the sweetest player in the world.'

'One day I am sweet, one day I am sour,' said the stranger.

O'Donnell was anxious to keep the stranger in his household, so he ordered twenty armed horsemen and twenty foot soldiers to guard him and positioned as many outside the gate.
'What are all these men for?' asked the stranger.
'To keep you here,' said O'Donnell.
'By my word, I shall not eat my supper here tomorrow, whatever you do.'
'If you stir one foot I will knock you to the ground,' said O'Donnell.

The stranger said nothing to this but took up his harp once more and played as sweetly as before. When they were all absorbed in the music, he shouted to the men outside: 'I'm coming out now. Watch carefully or you will lose me.'

The guards sprang into action and raised their axes to strike at him; but in their haste and confusion, somehow they only succeeded in hitting each other and in no time they all lay dead on the ground.

The stranger turned to O'Donnell. 'Now promise me twenty cows and a hundred acres of good land and I will bring your people back to life.'

Reluctantly O'Donnell agreed and the stranger delved in his bag, produced a bunch of fresh herbs and rubbed them on the mouth of each dead man. The guards woke up as whole and unharmed as ever—but when they looked around for the stranger, there was no sign of him to be seen.

The same stranger appeared in another household in Ireland, the house of Tadg O'Cealaigh. This time he showed the people a host of conjuring tricks and finally produced from his bag a thread of fine silk. He threw it up in the air so high it fastened itself in a cloud. Then the stranger delved into his bag and produced a hare which ran up the thread and disappeared. Next came a dog, which raced off after the hare and then a strong young serving boy. Last came a beautiful, well-dressed young woman.
'Follow them quickly,' said the stranger, 'but look out for the dog. He bites.'

Everyone stood looking up expectantly at the

cloud. At first they could hear the dog yelping after the hare, then everything went quiet.

'Something funny is going on up there,' said the stranger.

'What could it be?' they asked.

'I should say the dog is eating the hare and the boy is kissing the girl,' said the stranger and he pulled sharply on the thread. Down they all came, and it was just as he had said: the dog was just finishing off the bones of the hare and the boy had his arm round the girl and was kissing her.

'That's not right,' said the stranger and with one blow of his sword he struck off the boy's head.

'That's not right, either,' protested Tadg.

'Well I can soon *put* it right,' said the stranger and he picked up the boy's head and threw it at the body so that the two were joined together again. Unfortunately, however, the head was on back to front.

'He would be better dead than like that,' said Tadg.

'I can soon put it right,' said the stranger and in an instant he had twisted the head round and the boy was fit and well again.

Everyone was so busy looking at the boy that they quite forgot about the stranger—and when they turned back to him he had disappeared.

Mannanan travelled all around Ireland and no-one could keep him where he did not want to stay. Although his tricks were sometimes terrifying, he never harmed anyone but always revived them with his herbs and with his magic spells.

Mannanan's stronghold was on the summit of South Barrule Mountain, and when he was not on his travels he lived there, invisible to mortal eyes, shrouded in his magic mist. Whenever the island was threatened by enemy ships, he spread his mist over the whole of his kingdom, concealing it from hostile eyes. He could also make one man on the shore seem like an army of a hundred and could make wood chippings floating on the water appear to be a fleet of mighty warships. When the danger was past, he threw off his misty robes so that the sun warmed the land and the gorse and heather were musical with the hum of the bees. With such a protector, it is hardly surprising that the island was never invaded by the Romans and is still an independent and sovereign part of the United Kingdom.

The wonderful head

The pagan Celts were, like other northern people, head hunters who carried off the heads of their enemies as war trophies, displaying them proudly on the ramparts of their hillforts and in their houses. To the Celts, however, the heads were more than mere spoils of war for they believed that the head was the dwelling place of the soul, the very centre of a person's being. By displaying and worshipping the heads of their enemies they believed that they were gaining protection from the magical powers they possessed.

When real heads ceased to be used for religious purposes, replicas in stone, wood, metal and bone were made and were thought to have the same protective powers. The turnip lanterns of Hallowe'en (once the ancient feast day of Samain) is a substitute for the skull's head that would once have been used. No doubt in the Iron Age rush lights were put into the heads around the fortresses at this most sinister season of the Celtic year and very frightening they must have appeared as they glowed in the dark, ghostly night.

Heads were thought not only to keep evil at bay: they could also live on independently after the death of their owner's body. Some could talk, sing and prophesy. Water of every kind—wells, pools, river, lakes—was worshipped in Celtic times and if a head was placed in a sacred well it had a particularly strong magical effect. One tale tells of a fierce fight between two groups of Irishmen. Only one, Riach, survived and he cut off the heads of the dead men and took them to a well. The spring that fed the well instantly developed evil powers, bringing ill-luck to anyone who came near it. Riach built a well-house over the spring to try to contain the evil, then put a door across it and barred it firmly. But no force on earth could contain the violent malevolent water. It boiled and bubbled up inside the well, making the doors bulge with its pressure. Then suddenly it burst out with a roar, surging over the land around like a giant wave and drowning Riach and a thousand people round about.

Heads that lived on after their owners' deaths had powers for good as well as evil. Some, like the head of Bran in the story on page 69, presided over an Otherworld feast, providing food and drink and acting as host just as efficiently as when they were alive. Others brought murderers to justice by revealing their names. A human head played its own part in the great battle between Connacht and Ulster.

When Medb attacked the kingdom of Ulster in order to gain the brown bull of Cuailnge, the Ulster men were under the spell of a strange weakness which took away from them the will to fight. Only Cu Chulainn was unaffected and, alone, he challenged the might of the enemy army.

For many months he fought, battling in single combat against the best of Medb's heroes. At last, badly wounded and weary, he knew he could not continue for much longer.

One evening his human father Sualtaim found him lying exhausted, so weak and stiff from wounds that he could not bear the touch of his clothes and held them off with hazel-sticks, padded with layers of soft grass. The only place on his body without a wound was his left hand, which held his shield.

'How can I help you?' asked his father.

'Don't bother with me,' said Cu Chulainn. 'Go to the men of Ulster and tell them what is happening here. I cannot fight much longer. They must overcome their weakness and join with me or all Ulster will be lost.'

Sualtaim mounted Cu Chulainn's powerful grey warhorse and rode furiously to the palace of Emain Macha where the Ulster warriors lay idly feasting.

'Rouse yourselves, men of Ulster,' he shouted as he raced through the countryside. 'Men are dying, women are being carried away and cattle stolen while you sit by and do nothing. Shame on you!'

But the curse lay strong on the land of Ulster and they took no notice of Sualtaim's call.

At last he reached the fortress of Emain Macha itself and shouted out his terrible news again. Still there was no response. Not only were the men weak and uninterested; it was also forbidden for anyone to speak before the king gave the word and the king himself must not speak until Cathbad the druid had spoken. Three times Sualtaim shouted his fearful news before finally Cathbad looked up.

'Who is doing all this killing and this carrying away of women and this stealing of cattle?' he asked in an uninterested voice.

'Ailill and Medb have destroyed you,' shouted Sualtaim in a frenzy. 'Cu Chulainn alone is preventing the four kingdoms of Ireland from invading this land and you sit here uncaring. Stand up and fight like men for if you do not meet this attack now you will be utterly beaten and will be slaves until the day of doom.'

'Anyone who angers the king of Ulster like that is fit only to be killed,' said Cathbad with a yawn, turning back to his studies.

The others nodded in agreement but no-one showed any sign of taking action.

Angered by this useless answer, Sualtaim turned the great grey horse away sharply, pulling on its mane and driving his heels hard into its side in anger. Startled, the horse reared up on its hind legs and pawed the air with its hooves. As it did so, its neck struck Sualtaim's shield with such force that the sharp metal rim cut off his head and flung his body lifeless to the ground.

The frightened horse galloped back into the stockade, its eyes wide with terror and sweat foaming on its sides. On its back lay Sualtaim's shield and on the shield was his severed head. And all the time the head continued to cry out, 'Men are dying, women are being carried away and cattle stolen. Rouse yourselves, men of Ulster.'

At this fearful sight the curse which had brought weakness to the Ulster men was broken and they remembered who and what they were: the mighty warriors of Ulster.

Conchobar, the king, stood up then and swore a powerful oath: 'The heavens are over us, the earth beneath and the sea circles all around; I vow that unless the heavens fall with all their stars, and the earth gives way beneath us and the sea rises up to flood the whole land, I will restore every Ulster woman to her home and every Ulster cow to her stable.'

As the warriors sharpened their swords and prepared their long-forgotten armour, messengers were sent to rally men from every corner of the kingdom. Together a mighty force marched out to meet the enemy and save Cu Chulainn: the head of Sualtaim had done its work and could find peace at last.

Symbols in the Celtic myths and legends

At the beginning of each chapter the artist has illustrated some of the symbols and characters appearing in the stories.

TITLE PAGE A druid makes an offering to the gods using wooden images of the gods he is honouring. On the left the chalk figure of the Long Man of Wilmington dominates a Celtic hill fort which itself stands above a prehistoric stone circle. A magical druidic mist swirls over the landscape. The top border depicts some important Celtic animals; the bull, the deer, the boar, the horse goddess Epona, the swan and the dog; in its centre a double-headed god looks simultaneously at the living and at the dead. The bottom border shows Brigid, the goddess of poetry and fire; the sword which Arthur drew from the stone; the phases of the moon, representing the astronomical knowledge of the druids; Camelot, Arthur's legendary court; and Lir the god of the sea; in the centre two skulls represent the cult of the severed head. In the left-hand border are Celtic symbols of a plant (fertility) and chariot wheel (war) with typical Celtic representations of Danu the mother goddess, the Dagda, the father god, with his club and cauldron, and Nuada Silver Arm, a warrior god. The right-hand border shows the all-skilled god Lugh with his craftsmen's hammers, Cernunnos the horned god and the triple warrior goddess The Morrigan with her ravens.

p.11 THE ANCIENT CELTIC WORLD The designs at the top and bottom are adapted from a silver cauldron found at Gundestrup in Denmark and thought to be connected with the Irish story of the Cooley Cattle raid. They show a Celtic chieftain (top) and a Celtic queen with chariot wheels symbolizing her war-like character. In the centre is a Celtic helmet found in the River Thames and a dagger, with a simple Celtic hut and a cooking cauldron suspended by an iron chain. The framework of iron with its twisted links symbolizes the advances in metalwork which characterized Celtic civilization.

p.14 THE ARRIVAL OF THE GODS Top, the boats in which the people of Nemed reached Ireland and a wolf and venomous pig which helped them in battle. Below, the Tuatha de Danann and the Sons of Mil fight over the idyllic land of Ireland and divide it between them. Bottom, one of the *sidh* mounds which formed the entrances to the Otherworld of the Tuatha de Danann - originally burial mounds.

p.21 THE SECOND BATTLE OF MOYTURA Lugh the shining god throws a sling-shot into Balor's evil eye (top) whose lid has to be raised by force. Below, dead warriors killed in the battle are thrown into the healing well to be brought back to life.

p.25 THE SORROWS OF STORYTELLING Top, the tombstone of Cian the Mighty with his name inscribed in Ogam, the ancient 20-character alphabet made up of circles and lines meeting or crossing on the edge of a stone. Below, Cian in the shape of a pig. The one here is based on the so-called 'iron-age' breed, a cross between a domestic pig and a wild boar. Below this, Aoife the enchantress, herself transformed into a demon of the air, hovers over the Children of Lir in their swan forms. The golden chains around their necks indicate that they are really human beings.

p.32 THE STORY OF CU CHULAINN Cu Chulainn in his chariot with a Celtic shield decorated with typical stylized Celtic animals. Above and below are the two bulls which feature in the story: the Donn of Cuailnge (top) and the white-horned bull of Connacht.

p.53 THE STORY OF FIONN Fionn as the mythological protector of Ireland. In one hand he holds his spears, in the other his sling. Above and below are the deer and the duck he caught in his first hunting exploits, the shinty sticks and ball used in his boyhood trials of strength and the sacred salmon of knowledge.

p.65 THE FOUR BRANCHES OF THE MABINOGION From top to bottom: Pwyll and his hounds; the head of Bran, buried at the White Mount, the legendary site of the Tower of London; the army of mice who steal Manawydan's grain; the flowers from which Math and Gwydion created a wife for Lleu: meadow-sweet, oak and broom.

p.82 THE LEGEND OF KING ARTHUR The wizard Merlin conjures up visions of Arthur's life. Arthur as a boy pulls the sword from the anvil; Glastonbury tor (legendary site of Avallon, the Otherworld), with a circle symbolizing the Round Table and based on the design of the one now preserved in Winchester Castle; the last surviving knight watches as Arthur's body is borne away on the barge; the holy grail, the cup used at Jesus' last supper.

p.98 THE GODS OF THE PAGAN CELTS Two ravens, often shown as associates of the gods, perch beside an Irish wooden figure used as an offering. On the left is the father god, the Dagda with his club and magic cauldron; on the right Cernunnos, the horned god of fertility and plenty, pours out money from his purse. Beneath is a three-headed divinity from a terra-cotta vase made in the second century BC found in Bavay, France. Epona the horse goddess and a leprechaun (connected with Lugh, the patron god of shoemakers) are below and at the bottom are the leaves of the oak, a tree sacred to the druids.

p.104 MAGIC BIRDS AND ENCHANTED ANIMALS Entwined in the coils of a fire-breathing serpent are: Etain as a dragon-fly in her crystal cage; Cath Palug the monster cat; the crane, goose and cockerel which were tabu birds and could only be eaten at religious ceremonies; and a stag, associated with the horned god Cernunnos.

p.117 THE GIANTS OF MORVAH Bordered by a dry-stone wall (the 'giant's hedges' of Cornwall), Jack with his blackthorn staff strides over the hillside while the old giant gloats over his treasures deep below ground. Bottom, the people celebrate Morvah fair with festive fires and dancing around a stone cairn.

p.121 GODS OF THE LANDSCAPE The Wilmington Giant seen above three of the twelve mouthless stone heads found carved on a stone pillar at Entremont, France. Below, one of the mysterious sea women who bewitched Ruad and, beneath the head of the White Horse of Uffington, the three-legged emblem of the Isle of Man and the twelve stones that once stood on the plain of Mag Slecht.

p.128 THE WONDERFUL HEAD Symbols of the cult of the severed head, these are drawings of heads carved and modelled by Celtic craftsmen. Top left, head of a Celtic chieftain from Prague, Czechoslovakia; right, bronze head from Chartres, France. Below, carvings from Wakefield and Bradford, England. Below, the head on the shield is based on a decoration found on a horse harness. Bottom, the evil well of Riach bursts its walls to flood the land.

The main sources

Alcock, L., *Arthur's Britain*, Allen Lane 1971

Ashe, G., *A Guidebook to Arthurian Britain*, Longman 1980

Bottrell, W., *Hearthside Stories of West Cornwall*, Penzance 1870

Bromwich, Rachel, *The Triads of the Island of Britain*, University of Wales Press 1961, revised edition 1978

Cavendish, R., *King Arthur and The Grail*, Weidenfeld 1978

Comfort, W.W. (transl), *Arthurian Romances* by Chrétien de Troyes, London 1975

Cross, T.P. and Slover, C.H., *Ancient Irish Tales*, 1936

Dillon, M. and Chadwick, N.K., *The Celtic Realms*, Weidenfeld 1967

Ditmas, E.M.R., *Tristan and Iseult in Cornwall*, Forrester Roberts 1969

Fedrick, A.S. (transl), *The Romance of Tristan* by Beroul, Penguin 1970

Hunt, R., *Popular Romances of the West of England*, 1871

Jones, G. and Jones, T., *The Mabinogion*, Everyman 1975

Kinsella, T., *The Tain*, Oxford University Press 1972

MacCana, P., *Celtic Mythology*, Newnes 1970, revised edition 1984

MacNeill, M., *The Festival of Lughnasa*, Oxford University Press 1962

Malory, Sir Thomas, *Tales of King Arthur*, Guild Publishing 1980

Moore, A.W., *The Folklore of the Isle of Man*, 1891

Ross, A., *Everyday Life of the Pagan Celts*, Batsford 1970

Ross, A., *The Folklore of the Scottish Highlands*, Batsford hardback 1976, paperback 1986

Ross, A., *Pagan Celtic Britain*, Routledge and Kegan Paul 1967

Severin, T., *The Brendan Voyage*, Hutchinson 1978

Index

How to pronounce the names

In this book I have deliberately refrained from putting in the accents which occur in the academic texts, but have provided this list of principal places and characters to indicate how the names are pronounced in Old Irish and Welsh. These are only rough approximations as many of the sounds are unknown in the English language. The words have been separated into their syllables by hyphens to make pronunciation easier.

Aeb	Ayv	Dindshenchas	Deen-han-hus	Lleu Llaw Gyffes	Lhoo Lhou Kuff-es
Aed	A	Donn of Cuailnge	Down of Koo-ile-nyeh	Llyr	Lheer
Amergin	Ov-ar-gin	Duibhne	Die-nyeh	Luchta	Looh-ta
Angus	Een-us	Efnisien	Ave-nees-eye-yen	Lugh	Loo
Annwn	Ann-oo-in	Emer	Ay-ver	Macha	Moha
Aoife	If-e	Eochaid Airem	Yo-hi Ar-ev	Mag Murthemne	Moy Moor-hev-ne
Bendigeidfran	Ben-dig-ide-vran	Eremon	Ay-rev-on	Mag Slecht	Moy Slackd
Blodeuedd	Blod-oy-eth	Etain	Ayd-een	Matholwch	Math-ol-ook
Bodball	Bov-bal	Fiachra	Fe-ah-ra	Mathonwy	Math-on-oo-ee
Bodb Deargh	Bov Darg	Findbennach	Feen-ban-ah	Medb	May-v
Brian	Bree-an	Finneces	Fin-ayk-us	Miach	Mee-ah
Brigid	Bree-itch	Fionnachaidh	Fin-ah-hi	Midir	Mi-yar
Bri Leith	Bre La-ih	Fionnguala	Fin-goo-al-a	Mo Chaemoc	Mo Hay-voc
Caoilte mac Ronan	Kwel-che mok Ronan	Fionn mac Cumhall	Fin mok Koo-al	Nemed	Nev-eh
Cathbad	Kah-vah	Fomorian	Fo-vor-ee-an	Nuada	Noo-a-ha
Cei	Ky	Fuamnach	Foo-av-nah	O'Cealaigh	O-Kyal-eye
Cethan	Ke-han	Gilfaethwy	Gil-vyth-oo-ee	Ochall	O-hal
Cian	Kee-an	Goibniu	Goyv-ni-u	Oisin	Ush-een
Cu Chulainn	Koo Hoolin	Grainne	Gran-nyeh	Pwyll	Poo-ilh
Cynon	Ku-non	Ibar mac Riangabra	Ivar mok Re-an-govra	Riach	Ree-ah
Dagda	Doh-da	Iuchabar	Yew-ha-var	Samain	Sov-ain
Dechtire	Deh-ti-re	Iuchar	Yew-har	Sualtaim	Soo-al-tah
Diancecht	De-an-haht	Laeg	Loy-h	Tain bo Cuailnge	Tarn bow Koo-ile-nyeh
Diarmuid	De-ar-moo-id	Leborcham	Lyev-or-ham	Tuatha De Danann	Too-ah-ah Da Dan-an